The Earthrise Spirulina Cookbook

Make great meals with a superfood.

written and compiled by
Lance S. Sigal

authorHOUSE™
1663 Liberty Drive, Suite 200
Bloomington, Indiana 47403
(800) 839-8640
www.AuthorHouse.com

First published by AuthorHouse 02/24/05

ISBN: 1-4208-3655-2 (e)
ISBN: 1-4208-3654-4 (sc)

Library of Congress Control Number: 2005901698

Printed in the United States of America
Bloomington, Indiana

This book is printed on acid-free paper.

INTRODUCTION

2005 marks the 25th Anniversary of Earthrise Nutritionals, LLC as the worlds leading producer of Earthrise® Spirulina. As part of our Silver Anniversary Celebration, we've compiled many of the recipes that we've gathered over the past quarter of a century, as submitted by our team members as well as our customers.

Earthrise® is located in sunny, Southern California. Our "farm", where we grow all of our Earthrise® Spirulina, is located in Calipatria, California, a small farming community in the Sonoran Desert which is an hour and a half drive past Palm Springs and another hour to the Mexican-American border towns of Calexico – Mexicali. Our corporate Worldwide headquarters recently completed it's move to Irvine, California – a thirty minute drive to Anaheim (Home of Disneyland®).

We are proud of our past and excited about our future, with U.S Grown Spirulina being the most sought after Spirulina in the world because of the high quality of our product, including the facts that we are GMP Certified, ISO Certified, GRAS Affirmed, Kosher (KSA Certified) and we never irradiate our Earthrise® Spirulina. Quality is one of the keys to our success – we constantly test our Spirulina to ensure that the safety & quality statements as well as the nutritional values stated on our labels are accurate and truthful.

To learn more about Earthrise® and Earthrise® Spirulina, please visit our website at www.earthrise.com.

If you have a Spirulina recipe and want to share it with us, send it to recipes@earthrise.com and we'll send you some Earthrise® Spirulina to use in your life and cooking.

Dedications

To my wife, Saori, and my daughter, Luna, who mean the world to me.

and

To Ron Henson and Juan Chavez, who helped to create the first pond twenty-five years ago and provide the cornerstones for the company today and for the future.

FREE PRODUCTS

Do you have a favorite recipe that includes Earthrise® Spirulina and would like to see it included in the next edition of our cookbook? Simply e-mail it to recipes@earthrise.com. If we use your recipe, we'll send you a free bottle of an Earthrise® Spirulina product.

When you email your recipe, make sure that you include the following information:

- Name
- Address, City, State, Zip Code and Country
- Telephone Number (in case we have a question about your recipe)
- Email address

The Earthrise® Free Sample Program is open to residents of the United States and Canada. If you live outside of these areas, we can still use your recipe if you would like it included but will be unable to send a free bottle of our Spirulina.

Thank you,

The Earthrise Nutritionals Marketing Team

Table of Contents

What is Spirulina?

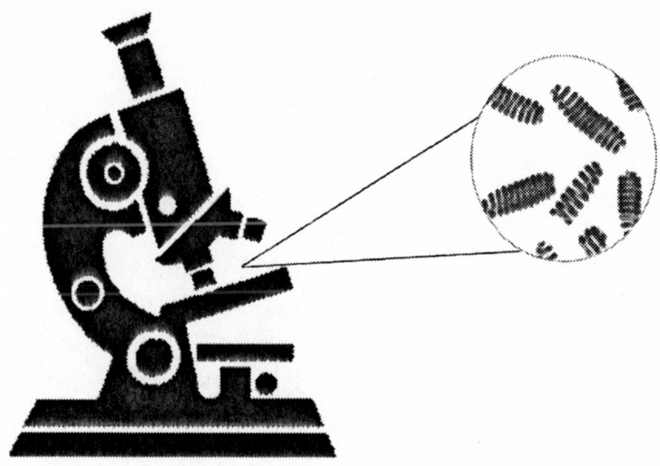

Earthrise® Spirulina is a green SuperFood for longevity and provides immune defense and natural antioxidant protection*

* These statements have not been evaluated by the Food and Drug Administration. This product is not intended to diagnose, treat, cure or prevent disease.

In technical terms, it's a blue-green alga, rich in phytonutrients, antioxidants, protein, vitamins and other nutrients & trace elements. In laypersons terms, it's a green Superfood that is rich in antioxidants and has an easily absorbed form of iron.

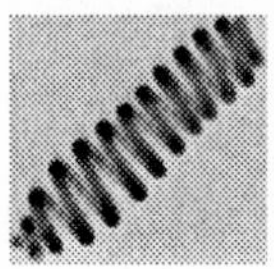

Earthrise® Spirulina has been grown in Southern California for twenty-five years, in highly controlled ponds to ensure the quality & safety of the Spirulina. It's sold in both bulk form to the commercial channel for use as a food ingredient and it's sold in a packaged form as a dietary supplement through various retail channels.

The packaged Spirulina is available in different formats (powder, tablets and capsules) as well as various color coded categories, including:

- EARTHRISE® Spirulina Natural® – a natural form of Spirulina which Promotes immune health and provides antioxidant benefits.*
- EARTHRISE® Spirulina Organic® – same benefits as EARTHRISE® Spirulina Natural®, but organically grown.
- EARTHRISE® Green Blends – Cleansing Formula – a cleansing formula which helps to detoxify the body naturally* with a revitalizing blend of EARTHRISE® Spirulina, Chlorella, Wheat Grass, Barley Grass, Alfalfa, and Broccoli.
- EARTHRISE® Green Blends - Light Appetite Formula – a proprietary, unique and natural formula for supporting weight maintenance*.
- EARTHRISE® Spirulina IL-4 – a natural Spirulina based proprietary formula which modulates the immune system and may reduce the IgE production.*
- EARTHRISE® Spirulina Digest & Flora Support – which provides an all-inclusive, proprietary formula of Spirulina, room temperature-stabile probiotic bacteria, digestive enzymes and prebiotic fructooligosaccharides (FOS) that work in harmony to support gastrointestinal function and immunity.*

* These statements have not been evaluated by the Food and Drug Administration.
This product is not intended to diagnose, treat, cure or prevent disease.

In additional, all of the Earthrise® packaged products are available in 30 & 60 day supply bottles – the powder format also has a bulk jar for "power" users and cooks.

Combined the color coded categories with the days supply and you have a simple, easy to use supplement program that can be used by anyone!

QUALITY is a critical issue for Earthrise®, as shown by the quality controls that we have implemented with various programs, including these symbols that you see on our packaging and literature (as applicable by category):

GRAS Affirmed – Earthrise has GRAS - "GRAS" is an acronym for the phrase **G**enerally **R**ecognized **A**s **S**afe. Under sections 201(s) and 409 of the Federal Food, Drug, and Cosmetic Act (the Act), any substance that is intentionally added to food is a food additive, that is subject to pre-market review and approval by FDA, unless the substance is generally recognized, among qualified experts, as having been adequately shown to be safe under the conditions of its intended use, or unless the use of the substance is otherwise excluded from the definition of a food additive. While it is impracticable to list all ingredients whose use is generally recognized as safe, FDA published a partial list of food ingredients whose use is generally recognized as safe to aid the industry's understanding of what did not require approval.

For more information on GRAS, please visit the FDA website at: http://www.cfsan.fda.gov/~dms/grasguid.html

Earthrise Nutritionals, LLC is an ISO9001 Registered Company

GMP (Good Manufacturing Practices) Certified Company

Certified Kosher

What are these things that have the asterisk (*) at the end of them?

These are called "Structure and Function Claims" (SFC's). The SFC is a specific claim made by a company regarding its product. The claim is made in regards to the effect of the product on structure and function of the human body.

It is important for consumers to understand several things about SFC's:

a) SFC's are not disease claims because dietary supplements are not intended to diagnose, treat, prevent or cure a disease. Rather, they are intended to support healthy structure and function of the body.

b) These claims must be substantiated by scientific evidence.

c) The FDA does not evaluate the substantiation of the claims but the language used to define the effect of the products. If the language is within that allowed for SFC, it will accept it; if not it will be rejected.

d) Though the evidence is not evaluated at the time of submission, the company is expected to have a documented evidence of the claim on file.

e) There should be an asterisk at the end of the claim that points to a disclaimer that is placed prominently on the label.

Earthrise Nutritionals, LLC. follows these FDA regulations covered by the Dietary Supplement Health and Education Act of 1994 (DSHEA).

For more information, please visit the F.D.A. website at www.fda.gov.

So, what does Spirulina really do for me?

The best way to answer this is to share the overall Nutritional Profile as shown on the next two pages.

For more great information on Earthrise® Spirulina, please visit our newly redesigned site at:

www.earthrise.com

Earthrise® Spirulina

NUTRITIONAL PROFILE [a]

Composition	Earthrise® Spirulina Tablets	% DV*	Earthrise® Spirulina Powder	% DV*
Serving Size	6 tabs (3 g)		3 g	
1. MACRONUTRIENTS [b]				
Calories	10		10	
Total Fat	0.2 g	< 2%	0.2 g	< 2%
Total Carbohydrate	0.5 g	< 2%	0.5 g	< 2%
Dietary Fiber	0.2 g	< 2%	0.2 g	< 2%
Protein	1.7 g	4%	1.7 g	4%
Essential Amino Acids				
Histidine	27 mg	**	27 mg	**
Isoleucine	95 mg	**	95 mg	**
Leucine	151 mg	**	151 mg	**
Lysine	89 mg	**	89 mg	**
Methionine	39 mg	**	39 mg	**
Phenylalanine	75 mg	**	75 mg	**
Threonine	83 mg	**	83 mg	**
Tryptophan	22 mg	**	22 mg	**
Valine	105 mg	**	105 mg	**
Non-Essential Amino Acids				
Alanine	123 mg	**	123 mg	**
Arginine	124 mg	**	124 mg	**
Aspartic Acid	170 mg	**	170 mg	**
Cystine	17 mg	**	17 mg	**
Glutamic Acid	275 mg	**	275 mg	**
Glycine	86 mg	**	86 mg	**
Proline	65 mg	**	65 mg	**
Serine	80 mg	**	80 mg	**
Tyrosine	69 mg	**	69 mg	**
2. VITAMINS [c]				
Vitamin A (as 100% □-Carotene)	4000 IU	80%	5,000 IU	100%
Vitamin K	16 mcg	20%	16 mcg	20%
Thiamine HCl (Vit. B-1)	0.004 mg	< 2%	0.004 mg	< 2%
Riboflavin (Vit. B-2)	0.08 mg	4%	0.08 mg	4%
Niacin (Vit. B-3)	0.43 mg	2%	0.43 mg	2%
Vitamin B-6 (Pyridox.HCl)	0.02 mg	< 2%	0.02 mg	< 2%
Vitamin B-12	2.8 mcg	45%	2.8 mcg	45%

Composition	**Earthrise® Spirulina Tablets**	% DV*	**Earthrise® Spirulina Powder**	% DV*
Serving Size	6 tabs (3 g)		3 g	
3. MINERALS [c]				
Calcium	13 mg	<2%	13 mg	<2%
Iron	1.7 mg	10%	1.7 mg	10%
Phosphorus	30 mg	2%	30 mg	2%
Iodine	1.2 mcg	< 2%	1.2 mcg	< 2%
Magnesium	9 mg	2%	9 mg	2%
Zinc	0.04 mg	<2%	0.04 mg	<2%
Selenium	0.6 mcg	<2%	0.6 mcg	<2%
Copper	10 mcg	<2%	10 mcg	<2%
Manganese	0.09 mg	4%	0.09 mg	4%
Chromium	2.8 mcg	2%	2.8 mcg	2%
Potassium	49 mg	<2%	49 mg	<2%
Sodium	15 mg	<2%	15 mg	<2%
4. PHYTONUTRIENTS [c]				
Phycocyanin	420 mg	**	420 mg	**
Chlorophyll	30 mg	**	30 mg	**
Gamma Linolenic Acid (GLA)	35 mg	**	35 mg	**
Total Carotenoids	8 mg	**	10 mg	**
b-Carotene	2.4 mg	**	3.0 mg	**
Zeaxanthin	2.0 mg	**	2.5 mg	**
Other Carotenoids	3.6 mg	**	4.5 mg	**

* Percent daily values are based on a 2,000 calorie diet.

**Percent daily values not established.

[a] This is a natural product and nutrient data may vary from one lot to another.

[b] Macronutrients data are based on most recent proximate analysis

[c] The data indicate minimum values observed.

TIPS & TRICKS

Cooking with Spirulina can be fun but challenging. Tips & Tricks include some great information on the best ways to cook with Spirulina as well as some extra recipes that can help supplement your cooking experience

WHY ADD THE SPIRULINA AS THE LAST INGREDIENT?

The natural consistency of Spirulina is unique in nature and not water soluble as many other foods, making it a bit sticky. By adding Spirulina as the last ingredient, especially in the blender, it's always best to add the Spirulina while the blender is moving (on a low speed) and be prepared to scrape down the sides of the blender to loosen any Earthrise® Spirulina powder that sticks.

CAN SPIRULINA BE COOKED?

Absolutely – however, keep in mind that cooking Spirulina, similar to cooking any vegetable, will reduce the nutritional content due to the heat. As you look through the recipes, you'll notice that Spirulina is usually added as the last item in order to reduce the amount of time that it's actually cooked.

The best way to illustrate this fact is this: place a small piece of broccoli into a glass dish. Put a bit of water in the dish and place it in the microwave for two to three minutes. Compare the cooked broccoli to the uncooked and you'll notice a difference in the shades of green – this is because of the heat and the reduction of the nutritional value.

WHAT IS TAHINI?

Tahini is sesame seed butter. To make tahini, sesame seeds are soaked in water for a day and then crushed to separate the bran from the kernels. The crushed seeds are put into salted water, where the bran sinks, but the kernels float and are skimmed off the surface. They are toasted, then ground to produce their oily paste. There are two types of tahini, light and dark, and the light ivory version is considered to have both the best flavor and texture.

TO MAKE TAHINI

2 cloves of garlic
Juice of 2 large lemons
6 Tablespoons of Sesame Seeds
Pinch of ground cumin
1 teaspoon freshly chopped parsley

Step-By-Step Instructions:

Crush the garlic and salt together. Mix with a little lemon juice and blend with the mixture. Add the cumin and remaining lemon juice to form a smooth paste, like peanut butter.

Use additional garlic if you want the tahini to taste stronger. If it is too thick, loosen it with a little water.

TO MAKE COCONUT CREAM

There is one recipe that calls for coconut cream . . . should you choose to make your own coconut cream, it's very easy and this is all that you have to do:

- 1 Fresh Coconut
- 3/4 Cup of Warm Water

- Break the coconut in half
- Carefully remove the coconut meat from the shell and place into a blender
- Add the water
- Blend the mixture until the coconut and water are well combined
- Pour into a sieve and slowly squeeze the liquid out
- The residue will result in approximately 1-½ to 2 Cups of Coconut Cream

WHAT IS SHOYU?

Shoyu is the Japanese word for Soy Sauce. You can buy soy sauce from almost any grocery store or health food store – our recommendation is to use the regular, although you can use the low sodium version if you need to watch your intake sodium.

WHAT IS TAMARI?

Tamari is a thicker version of Shoyu (soy sauce). Tamari is available at many health food stores and some grocery stores. You can substitute Shoyu in place of Tamari.

BREAKFAST

Breakfast is the first meal of the day.

Earthrise® Spirulina has a high concentration of Phycocyanin. Phycocyanin is important because of its antioxidant and anti-inflammatory activities. It may also be important in blood cell regeneration and detoxification.*

* These statements have not been evaluated by the Food and Drug Administration. This product is not intended to diagnose, treat, cure or prevent disease.

TOFU OMELETE

- 6 Large Eggs
- 2 Medium Tomatoes, Thickly Sliced
- 1/3 Pound Tofu, Mashed
- 1 Cup Jack or Cheddar Cheese, Grated
- 2 Tablespoons of Chopped Green Onion
- 1 Tablespoon of Earthrise® Spirulina
- 1 Tablespoon of Sesame Seeds (Optional)
- 1 teaspoon Shoyu
- Sliced Mushrooms (Optional)
- Pepper (to Taste)

- Put a frying pan over a low heat on the stove
- Lightly beat the eggs in a mixing bowl
- Add all of the remaining ingredients (except the tomatoes) and then mix well
- Pour the mixture into the frying pan and whisk until the cheese is slightly melted and the eggs are cooked to your liking
- Serve on a serving plate with the tomatoes as a garnish.
- Sprinkle the sesame seeds over the dish to provide an earthy, nutty crunch.

This breakfast offers approximately four (4) servings.

EGGS SPIRATINE

- 6 Medium Eggs
- 1 Large Tomato, Thickly Sliced
- 1-½ Pounds of Fresh Spinach
- 1–1/2 Cups of Milk
- 1/4 Cup of Flour
- 3 Ounces of Grated Parmesan Cheese
- 2 Ounces of Butter
- 3 Tablespoons of Light Cream
- 1 Tablespoon of Earthrise® Spirulina
- 1/2 teaspoon of Celery Salt
- 1/2 teaspoon of Seasoned Salt
- 1 Dash of Salt

- Preheat the oven to 375°
- Wash the spinach and chop into big pieces and place into a medium bowl, sprinkling the salt over it
- Mix the spinach with half of the butter, the seasonings and the Earthrise® Spirulina
- Put the mixture into an over-proof dish
- Make the cheese sauce by melting the remaining butter in a saucepan over a low heat
- Blend the flour into the cheese until completely mixed and then cook for another minute
- Turn the heat off, slowly pour the milk into the pan while constantly stirring and then bring to a boil, still constantly stirring
- Cook for another 2 minutes
- Stir in a little more than half of the cheese and take the pan off of the stove
- Poach the eggs lightly then arrange on the spinach in the oven-proof dish
- Add the cream to the cheese sauce and then pour over the spinach and the eggs
- Sprinkle the remaining cheese over the eggs
- Bake in the oven until golden brown (about 10 minutes)
- Arrange the tomato slices on the eggs

This main dish serves six (6) people.

SNACKS

Athletes often exercise too much – much more than the normal exercise required to maintain good health. Under such circumstances, some imbalance in immune system function can occur. Earthrise® Spirulina may help balance the immune system function. Through its function in modulating the immune system, Earthrise® Spirulina may increase energy, endurance and stamina in athletes.*

* These statements have not been evaluated by the Food and Drug Administration. This product is not intended to diagnose, treat, cure or prevent disease.

SUNFLOWER SNACKERS

- 2 Cups of Natural Raw Sunflower Seeds
- 2 teaspoons of Earthrise® Spirulina
- 1/2 teaspoon Shoyu
- 1/2 teaspoon of Vegetable Broth Mix
- A Dash of Cayenne to Taste

- Place all of the ingredients into a plastic bag
- Shake vigorously
- Pour into a serving bowl

This snack offers approximately one (1) serving.

GREEN POTATO CHIPS

- 6 Red Skin Potatoes
- 2 Tablespoons Earthrise® Spirulina
- 3 teaspoons Tamari
- 2 teaspoons Paprika
- 1 teaspoon Cumin Powder
- 1 Dash Virgin Olive Oil

- Preheat the over to 375°
- Slice the potatoes lengthwise into thin strips
- Drizzle the olive oil over the slices and toss until evenly coated
- Sprinkle the spices over the potato slices and toss again until evenly coated
- Bake on a cookie sheet until golden brown – turning the potato slices several times

This snack offers approximately Four (4) servings.

GREEN TOASTERS

- 2 – 10" Loaves of Fresh French Bread
- 2 Garlic Cloves (Crushed)
- 1-1/2 Cups of Butter
- 1 Cup Sesame Seeds
- 2 Tablespoons of Earthrise® Spirulina
- 1/2 teaspoon of Fresh Thyme
- Pepper (to Taste)
- Salt (to Taste)

- Pre-heat the oven to 400°
- Using a small sauce-pan, melt the butter, garlic, thyme, and pepper over a low heat as to not to burn the butter.
- Remove the garlic and then discard it
- Whip in the Earthrise® Spirulina
- Cut the bread into ½" to ¾" slices
- Dip one side of each slice of bread into the Earthrise® Spirulina & butter mix
- Spread the sesame seeds onto a plate and coat the side of each slice of bread with a thin coat of the seeds
- After coating each slice of bread, place them face-up on a baking sheet
- Bake for approximately 25 – 30 minutes or until they are lightly toasted
- Arrange them on a wooden bread-board or a medium serving platter
- Garnish with parsley sprigs

This snack offers approximately six to eight (6 - 8) servings.

POPPED EARTHRISE® SPIRULINA

- 8 Ounces of Pre-Popped Popcorn (Works Best on Oiled or Buttered Popcorn)
- 3 Tablespoons of Earthrise® Spirulina
- 4 teaspoons of Nutritional or Brewers Yeast
- 2 teaspoons of Spike Seasoning
- Your Favorite Herbs, including chili powder
- Salt (To Taste)
- Butter

- Place the popcorn into a large bowl
- Sprinkle all of the other ingredients over the popcorn
- Using two large spoons, carefully toss the popcorn until completely covered

This snack offers approximately One to Two (1-2) servings.

BEVERAGES

Increase antioxidant protection. Natural antioxidants in Earthrise® Spirulina clean up excess free radicals and may prevent premature aging.*

* These statements have not been evaluated by the Food and Drug Administration. This product is not intended to diagnose, treat, cure or prevent disease.

MORNING BLASTOFF

- 1-½ Cups Frozen Blueberries
- 1 Container Vanilla Yogurt (Approximately 6 Ounces)
- 1-1/2 Cups Frozen Blackberries
- 1/2 Cup Orange Juice
- 2 Tablespoons Toasted Wheat Germ
- 2 Tablespoons Honey
- 1 Tablespoon Earthrise® Spirulina

- Blend all but the Earthrise® Spirulina into a blender
- Next, blend the Earthrise® Spirulina into mixture
- Pour into glasses

This beverage offers two (2) servings.

GREEN SMOOTHIE

- 1 Fresh Banana (Slightly Green)
- 1 Fresh Peach
- 1 Fresh Pear
- 1 Glass Pineapple Juice
- 2 Tablespoons of Grapenuts® Cereal
- 1 Tablespoon of Earthrise® Spirulina
- Honey (To Taste) – Optional

- Blend the first four ingredients in a blender
- Next, blend the Earthrise® Spirulina into mixture
- Pour into two (2) chilled glasses
- Sprinkle the cereal over the top

This beverage offers two (2) servings.

BLUE-GREEN SMOOTHIE

- 3 Cups of Organic Apple Juice
- 3 Fresh Bananas (Slightly Green)
- 1/2 Cup of Blueberries (Fresh or Frozen)
- 2 Tablespoons of Bran
- 1-1/2 Tablespoons of Earthrise® Spirulina

- Blend all but the Earthrise® Spirulina into a blender
- Next, blend the Earthrise® Spirulina into mixture
- Pour into 3 glasses

This beverage offers three (3) servings.

TROPICAL SPIRAL

- 2 Dates
- 1 Medium Mango, Peeled & Pitted
- 1 Six (6) Ounce Package Silken Tofu
- 1- 1/2 Cups Vanilla Soy Milk
- 1 Cup Frozen Raspberries
- 1 Tablespoon Earthrise® Spirulina

- Blend all but the Earthrise® Spirulina into a blender
- Next, blend the Earthrise® Spirulina into mixture
- Pour into tall glasses

This beverage offers two (2) servings.

SPIRU-APPLE JUICE

- 3 Cups of Organic Apple Juice
- 1-1/2 Tablespoons of Earthrise® Spirulina
- 1/2 teaspoon of Cinnamon
- 1/4 teaspoon of Nutmeg

- Blend all of the ingredient into a blender
- Blend well
- Pour into chilled glasses

This beverage offers three (3) servings.

MAJOR GREEN POWER

- 1-1/2 Cup Apple Juice
- 2 Bananas, Peeled
- 1/2 Cup Frozen Blueberries
- 1/2 Cup Fresh Peach Slices
- 1/2 Cup Cherries, Pitted
- 2 Tablespoons Earthrise® Spirulina
- 1/2 teaspoon Royal Jelly
- Ice Cubes

- Blend all but the Earthrise® Spirulina into a blender
- Next, blend the Earthrise® Spirulina into mixture
- For a thicker concoction, use more ice
- Pour chilled classes

This beverage offers three - four (3-4) servings.

GREEN FUEL

- 1 Kiwi, Peeled
- 1 Banana, Peeled
- 1 Medium Orange, Peeled
- 1 Cup Non-Sweetened Apple Juice
- 3/4 Cup Plain Yogurt
- 3 Tablespoons Pumpkin Seeds, Shelled
- 2 Tablespoons Earthrise® Spirulina
- 1 Tablespoon Aloe Vera Juice
- 1 teaspoon Flax Seeds

- Blend pumpkin & flax seeds with half of the juice for 20 – 30 seconds
- Add the remaining ingredients and blend for 1 minute
- Blend all but the Earthrise® Spirulina into a blender
- Next, blend the Earthrise® Spirulina into mixture
- For a thicker concoction, use more ice
- Pour into tall, chilled glasses

This beverage offers three (3) servings.

THE POWER OF GREEN

- 2 Celery Stalks, Cleaned
- 1/2 Lemon
- 1-1/2 Cups Tomato Juice
- 2 Tablespoons Earthrise Spirulina
- 1/2 teaspoon Garlic Granules
- 1/4 teaspoon Horseradish
- 1 Dash Salt
- 1 Dash Ground Black Pepper
- 1 Dash Hot Sauce

- Blend all but the Earthrise® Spirulina and lemon into a blender
- Next, blend the Earthrise® Spirulina into mixture
- Pour into tall glasses
- Put a slice of lemon and a celery stalk into each drink

This beverage offers two (2) servings.

CAROB MALT

- 2 Dates
- 1 Banana, Peeled
- 1-1/2 Cup Soy Milk
- 2 Tablespoons Carob Powder
- 2 Tablespoons Tahini
- 1 teaspoon Vanilla
- 1 teaspoon Earthrise® Spirulina

- Blend all but the Earthrise® Spirulina into a blender
- Next, blend the Earthrise® Spirulina into mixture
- Pour into tall, chilled glasses

This beverage offers two (2) servings.

TWISTED SPIRULINA

- 1 Cup Fresh Orange Juice
- 1 Banana, Peeled
- 2 Tablespoons Earthrise Spirulina
- 4 Frozen Strawberries
- 1 teaspoon of Fresh Lime Juice
- Ice

- Blend all but the Earthrise® Spirulina into a blender
- Next, blend the Earthrise® Spirulina into mixture
- For a thicker concoction, use more ice
- Pour into chilled glasses
- Use rind peelings from the orange and lime for garnish

This beverage offers three (3) servings.

CARIBBEAN SMOOTHIE

- 3 Cups of Pineapple Juice
- 1 Cup of Coconut Cream (See Recipe in Tips & Tricks or use a can from the store)
- 2 Tablespoons of Cherry Syrup
- 2 Tablespoons of Wheat Germ
- 1 Tablespoon of Brewers Yeast
- 1 Tablespoon of Earthrise® Spirulina

- Blend all but the Earthrise® Spirulina into a blender
- Next, blend the Earthrise® Spirulina into mixture
- Pour into chilled glasses

This beverage offers three (3) servings.

AFTER-HOUR BEVERAGES

Earthrise® Spirulina supports immune function by enhancing the activity of natural killer (NK) cells.*

* These statements have not been evaluated by the Food and Drug Administration. This product is not intended to diagnose, treat, cure or prevent disease.

FROZEN SPIRULINA SCREWDRIVER

- 3 Shots Vodka
- 2 Cups Fresh Orange Juice
- 2 Tablespoons Earthrise® Spirulina
- Ice

- Blend all but the Earthrise® Spirulina into a blender
- Next, blend the Earthrise® Spirulina into mixture
- Pour into highball glasses
- For a thicker concoction, use more ice

This beverage offers two (2) servings.

CREAMY SPIRUTINY

- 1 Banana, Peeled
- 1 Shot Gin
- 1-1/2 Cup Soy Milk
- 2 Tablespoons Pumpkin Seeds, Shelled
- 2 Tablespoons Earthrise® Spirulina
- 2 Tablespoons Almond Butter

- Blend all but the Earthrise® Spirulina into a blender
- Next, blend the Earthrise® Spirulina into mixture
- Pour into martini glasses

This beverage offers two to three (2 - 3) servings.

DOUBLE THE POWER OF GREEN

- 2 Celery Stalks, Cleaned
- 2 Shots Vodka
- 1/2 Lemon
- 1-1/2 Cups Tomato Juice
- 2 Tablespoons Earthrise® Spirulina
- 1/2 Teaspoon Garlic Granules
- 1/4 Teaspoon Horseradish
- 1 Dash Salt
- 1 Dash Ground Black Pepper
- 1 Dash Hot Sauce

- Blend all but the Earthrise® Spirulina and lemon into a blender
- Next, blend the Earthrise® Spirulina into mixture
- Pour into tall glasses
- Put a slice of lemon and a celery stalk into each drink

This beverage offers two to three (2 - 3) servings.

DIPS

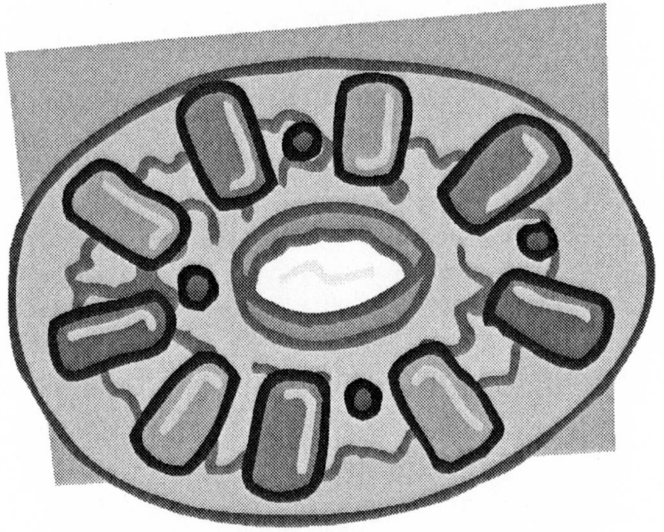

Reduce the negative effects of the body's normal inflammatory response. Inflammation is the body's first line of defense against foreign attack, but when it goes unchecked, it leads to conditions that promote premature aging. Antioxidants in Earthrise® Spirulina clean up the free radicals that are produced during normal inflammatory response.*

* These statements have not been evaluated by the Food and Drug Administration. This product is not intended to diagnose, treat, cure or prevent disease.

CREAMY AVOCADO DIP

- 2 Large Ripe Avocado
- 1 Lemon, Juiced
- 1 Small Tomato, Finely Diced
- 1/2 Fresh Grated Onion
- 1/3 of a Cup of Sour Cream
- 1 Tablespoon of Mayonnaise
- 1/2 Tablespoon of Earthrise® Spirulina
- 2 teaspoons of Fresh Minced Garlic
- 1/4 teaspoon Hot Sauce
- Pepper (To Taste)
- Fresh "Dipping" Veggies, Cut into Strips

- Peel the avocado and remove the pit
- In a blender, purée the avocado, sour cream, mayonnaise, lemon juice, garlic, onion, pepper and Earthrise® Spirulina
- Pour the purée into a serving bowl
- Cut the tomato into small pieces and garnish the edges of the bowl
- Arrange the "Dipping" Veggies on a platter.

This dip offers approximately two (2) cups.

SALTY AVOCADO DIP

- 2 Cloves of Fresh Garlic
- 1 Large Ripe Avocado
- 1 Pound of Sour Cream
- 1 Tablespoon of Earthrise® Spirulina
- Your Favorite Herbs
- Pepper (To Taste)
- Fresh "Dipping" Veggies, Cut into Strips

- Peel the avocado and remove the pit
- In a blender, purée all of the ingredients except the Earthrise® Spirulina
- Next, blend in the Earthrise® Spirulina
- Pour the purée into a serving bowl
- Arrange the "Dipping" Veggies on a platter.

This dip offers approximately three (3) cups.

TAN & GREEN DIP

- 12 Almonds
- 6 Fresh Garlic Cloves
- 3 Green Onions, Chopped
- 1 Lemon, Juiced
- 1 Cup of Parsley
- 4 Tablespoons Nutritional Yeast
- 3 Tablespoons Tamari
- 2 Teaspoons Earthrise® Spirulina
- 1 Tablespoon of Fresh Ginger, Grated
- Warm Water

- De-shell the almonds and soak them in water overnight
- Drain the water
- Place everything in a blender
- Pour enough water in the blender to cover everything
- Blend until smooth
- Add salt and pepper to taste
- Chill

This dip offers approximately one & one half (1-1/2) cups.

GUACAMOLE DIP

- 2 Large Ripe Avocados
- 2 to 4 Green Chili Peppers, with the Seeds Removed (Suggested – Serrano Chili's)
- 1 Small Tomato, Cut into Small Pieces
- 1 Bag of Corn Chips
- 1/4 of a Medium Onion
- 2 Tablespoons of Fresh Lemon Juice
- 1 Tablespoon of Earthrise® Spirulina
- 3/4 teaspoon of Salt

- Peel the avocados and remove the pit
- In a large bowl, blend all of the ingredients except some of the tomato
- Sprinkle the rest of the tomato on top of the mixture

This dip offers approximately two (2) cups.

SPREADS

Antioxidants, such as the ones in Earthrise® Spirulina, help to protect the body from the damaging effects of free radicals.*

* These statements have not been evaluated by the Food and Drug Administration.
This product is not intended to diagnose, treat, cure or prevent disease.

SPIRULINA SUPER SPREAD

- 1 Can of Anchovy Fillets (2 ounces) – Drained
- 1 Garlic Clove
- 1 Small Loaf of French or Sour Dough Bread
- ¾ of a Cup Virgin Olive Oil
- 2 Tablespoons of Fresh Lemon Juice
- 1 Tablespoon of Earthrise® Spirulina
- 1 teaspoon of a Dijon type Mustard
- 1 teaspoon of Thyme (Dried)
- ¼ teaspoon of Basil (Dried)
- A Pinch of White Pepper

- Combine all of the ingredients (except the oil) in a blender and cover
- Blend on a higher speed for approximately 30 to 40 seconds
- Keeping the blender on high, carefully remove the cover, then very slowly pour the oil into the mixture
- Continue blending the mixture for another 2 to 3 minutes
- Pour the mixture into a small bowl
- Cut the bread into thin slices
- Spread the dip onto the bread slices

* Healthy Option: Use the spread as a dip with Fresh Cut Veggies

This spread offers approximately one (1) cup.

SALMON SPIRULINA MOUSSE

- 1 Packaged of Unflavored Gelatin Powder
- 1 Small Cucumber
- 1 Small Tomato
- ¼ Pound of Fresh Salmon
- ½ Cup of Heavy Cream, Whipped into a Foamy State
- ½ Cup of Boiling Water
- ½ Cup of Mayonnaise
- ¼ Cup of Cold Water
- 2 Tablespoon of Earthrise® Spirulina
- 1 Tablespoon of Fresh Lemon Juice
- 1 Tablespoon Grated Onion
- 1 Teaspoon of Salt
- ½ Teaspoon of Hot Sauce

- In a large mixing bowl, sprinkle the gelatin powder into the cold water
- Next, add the boiling water and stir until dissolved
- Let the bowl sit for 5 minutes
- Add the mayonnaise, lemon juice, onion, hot sauce, salt and Earthrise® Spirulina to the gelatin
- Mix until fully combined
- Chill until the gelatin sets to a creamy consistency
- In a small frying pan, cook the fish with a little oil until pink all of the way through the fillet
- Place the fish into the blender and purée into a fine paste
- Carefully mix the salmon into the gelatin mixture
- Next, carefully mix the whipped cream into the mixture
- Pour into a gelatin mold and refrigerate overnight
- Once chilled, "pop" the salmon mixture from the mold onto a serving dish
- Peel and cut the cucumbers & tomatoes into thin slices (for garnish)

* Healthy Option: Serve with whole wheat crackers

This spread offers approximately six to eight (6 - 8) servings.

APPETIZERS

Studies have shown that phytonutrients, like phycocyanin in Earthrise® Spirulina, modulate the immune system.*

* These statements have not been evaluated by the Food and Drug Administration.
This product is not intended to diagnose, treat, cure or prevent disease.

STUFFED MUSHROOMS

- 8 to 10 Large Mushrooms
- 1 Pound of Fresh Carrots (Peeled and Sliced into ¼" Thick Sticks)
- 1 Small White Onion (Diced as Fine as Possible)
- ¼ Cup of Butter
- 2 Tablespoon of Orange Marmalade
- 1 Tablespoon of Lemon Juice
- 1 Teaspoon of Curry Powder
- ½ Teaspoon of Earthrise® Spirulina
- ¼ Teaspoon of Ginger Powder

- Remove the stems from the mushroom caps and sauté in the butter and lemon over a medium heat until lightly browned
- Cook carrots in a pot of salted water until tender (seven to ten minutes)
- Drain the water and stir the ginger powder with the carrots
- Purée the carrots in a blender
- Mix the marmalade, onion, curry and Spirulina together and divide evenly between the mushroom caps, filling each one about half full
- Use a small spoon to fill the rest of the space in each cap – a pastry bag may be used if you have one
- You may refrigerate the filled mushroom caps for a few hours if they are to be made in advance
- Pre-heat the oven to 350°
- Bake the mushrooms for 10 minutes or until thoroughly heated

* Healthy Options: Sprinkle the tops of each mushroom with a pinch of finely chopped parsley for color contrast.

This appetizer offers eight to ten (8 - 10) servings.

COD FRITTERS

- Batter
    - 1/3 Cup White Flour
    - 1/3 Cup of Warm Water
    - 1/3 Teaspoon Baking Powder
- Filling
    - 1/2 Pound of Salted Cod (or any other salted white fish)
    - 2 Garlic Cloves
    - 1/8 Cup of Earthrise® Spirulina
    - 4 Tablespoons of Fresh Chopped Parsley
    - 1/2 teaspoon Cayenne Pepper
    - 1 Dash of Salt
- Tarter Sauce
    - 4 Hardboiled Eggs
    - 4 Tablespoons of Mayonnaise
    - 4 teaspoons Rice Wine
    - 4 teaspoons of Vinegar

- Soak the fish in the refrigerator overnight
- The next day, flake or shred the fish
- In a medium to large sized mixing bowl, combine the batter ingredients and mix well
- Add one cup of the cod (well packed) along with the parsley, garlic, Spirulina, cayenne and the salt
- Mix all of these ingredients well
- Turn on the deep fryer OR fill a small pot with vegetable oil and heat on a medium heat. Test the oils temperature by putting a drop of the batter into the oil – when it rises to the top, the temperature is ready
- Carefully drop spoonfuls of the batter mixture into the oil and fry until each fritter rises to the surface of the oil
- As each fritter is ready, take it from the oil and let it drain on some paper towels
- To make the tarter sauce, Separate the white and yellow sections of the egg
- Chop the white part into fine pieces
- In a bowl, combine the other ingredients and mix well
- Mix in the chipped egg whites

This appetizer offers ten to twelve (10 - 12) servings.

SAUCES & GRAVYS

Eat your Earthrise® Spirulina greens for good health!*

* These statements have not been evaluated by the Food and Drug Administration. This product is not intended to diagnose, treat, cure or prevent disease.

JAPANESE SPIRULINA SAUCE

- 1 Pound of Firm Tofu
- 1 Tablespoon Earthrise® Spirulina
- 1 Tablespoon of Miso
- 1 teaspoon of Shoyu (Soy Sauce)
- 1 teaspoon of Sake (Rice Wine)

- Combine all of the ingredients in a blender and cover
- Blend on a higher speed for approximately 30 to 40 seconds

* Healthy Options: Use as a salad dressing or a dip for fresh cut veggies

This sauce offers approximately one (1) cup.

INDIAN SPIRULINA SAUCE

- 2 Medium Avocados
- 1 Tablespoon of Earthrise® Spirulina
- 3/4 teaspoon of Curry Powder
- Other Spices to Taste

- Combine all of the ingredients in a blender and cover
- Blend on a higher speed for approximately 30 to 40 seconds

* Healthy Options: Use as a salad dressing or a dip for fresh cut veggies

This sauce offers approximately one and a half (1-1/2) cups.

SPIRULINA GRAVY

- 5 Fresh Garlic Cloves, Crushed
- ½ Cup Rice Flour
- 4 Tablespoons Tamari
- 3 Tablespoons Brewers Yeast
- 1 Tablespoon Earthrise® Spirulina
- 1 teaspoon Cumin Powder
- Warm Water

- Slowly brown the rice flour in a small saucepan over a medium heat, stirring constantly until slightly brown
- Slowly add a little water at a time, while mixing, until thick
- Add the remaining ingredients (except Spirulina) and simmer over a low heat for 5 minutes
- Add a little more water if needed (mixture should be pourable)
- Whisk in the Spirulina

* Healthy Options: Ad two finely sliced mushrooms

This sauce offers approximately one (1) cup.

SPIRULINA TOFU GRAVY

- 3 Fresh Lemons, Juice Only
- 1 Package Soft Tofu
- 1/3 Cup Brewers Yeast
- 1/4 Cup Fresh Parsley, Shredded
- 3 Tablespoons Lecithin
- 3 Tablespoons Fresh Ginger, Grated
- 2 Tablespoons Paprika
- 1 Tablespoon Earthrise® Spirulina
- 1 Tablespoon Tamari

- Blend all of the ingredients into a blender
- Using a medium setting, blend until creamy (add a bit of water if too thick)
- Heat over a low heat until warm
- Serve over steamed vegetables or Tofu Cutlets

* Healthy Options: Substitute ¼ Cup Fresh Basil (Shredded) for the parsley

This sauce offers approximately two (2) cups.

APPLE-SPIRULINA SAUCE

- 5 Large Red Apples
- 1/4 Cup of Almonds, Crushed
- 1 Tablespoon of Earthrise® Spirulina
- 1/2 teaspoon of Lemon Juice
- 1/2 teaspoon of Cinnamon
- 1/4 teaspoon of Nutmeg

- Cut the apples into small sections and remove the cores/ seeds
- Put some water into a small saucepan
- Put all of the ingredients, except the Earthrise® Spirulina, into the saucepan
- Cook over a low heat until the apples are soft
- Pour the mixture into a blender and blend until it is fairly smooth

* Healthy Options: Use green apples for a tart taste

This sauce offers approximately six (6) servings.

PESTO PASTA SAUCE

- 1 Garlic Clove
- 1/2 Cup Parmesan Cheese, Grated
- 1/4 Cup Virgin Olive Oil
- 1/4 Cup Butter
- 1 Tablespoon Fresh Parsley, Chopped
- 1 Tablespoon Earthrise® Spirulina
- 1 Tablespoon Fresh Basil
- 1 teaspoon Lemon Juice
- 1 Dash Freshly Ground Black Pepper

- Combine all of the ingredients (except Spirulina) in a blender
- Blend until smooth, hen add the Spirulina
- Serve the sauce over freshly cooked pasta

* Healthy Options: Add a bit of cilantro for a spicier taste

This sauce offers approximately four (4) servings.

GREEK SPIRULINA SAUCE

- 1/3 of a Pound of Feta Cheese
- 1/2 Garlic Clove, Minced
- 3 Cups of Spinach Leaves, Chopped Finely
- 1 Cup of Plain Yogurt
- 1/4 Cup of Black Olives, Chopped Finely
- 3 Tablespoons of Green Onion, Chopped Finely
- 1 Tablespoon of Earthrise® Spirulina
- 1 Dash of Cayenne
- Salt to Taste

- Mash the feta cheese through a fine sieve and into a bowl
- Mix in the yogurt and combine the two ingredients thoroughly
- Mix in the rest of the ingredients
- Put the mixture into a serving bowl
- Chill for an hour before serving

* Healthy Options: Use as a dip with pita bread that has been cut into strips and toasted or with fresh cut veggies. Also use as a salad dressing.

This sauce offers approximately one and a half (1-1/2) cups.

SALADS & DRESSINGS

Eating your Earthrise® Spirulina greens promotes good health!*

* These statements have not been evaluated by the Food and Drug Administration. This product is not intended to diagnose, treat, cure or prevent disease.

SPIRULINA SPROUT SALAD

- 1 Garlic Clove, Minced
- 2 Cups of Fresh Bean Spouts
- 1/4 Cup of Green Onion, Minced
- 1/4 Cup of Pimento, Finely Chopped
- 1/4 Cup of Virgin Olive Oil
- 2 Tablespoons of White Vinegar
- 2 Tablespoons of Shoyu
- 2 Tablespoons Ground White Sesame Seeds
- 2 teaspoons Earthrise® Spirulina
- 1 teaspoon of Clover Honey
- ½ teaspoon of Salt
- ½ teaspoon of Ground Black Pepper

- Mix everything except for the bean sprouts together in a medium mixing bowl
- Rinse the bean sprouts and place in a serving bowl
- Pour the seasonings over the bean sprouts and toss

* Healthy Options: Garnish with crispy onions.

This salad offers four to five (4 - 5) servings.

GREEN CREAMY DRESSING

- 1 Small Avocado, Peeled, Pitted & Cubed
- 1/2 Clove Garlic
- 1/2 Cup of Heavy Cream
- 1/4 Cup of Olive Oil
- 3 Tablespoons of Fresh Lemon Juice
- 3 Tablespoons of Fresh Green Onion, Minced
- 2 Tablespoons Earthrise® Spirulina
- 1 teaspoon of Dill
- 1/2 teaspoon of Sea Salt
- 1/2 teaspoon of Fresh Ground Pepper

- Place all of the ingredients into a blender until smooth

* Healthy Options: Add some thyme or basil for different flavor variations

This dressing offers approximately eight (8) servings.

CREAMY GREEN DRESSING

- 3 Tablespoons Mayonnaise
- 2 Tablespoons Plain Yogurt
- 2 Tablespoons of White Onion, Minced
- 1 Tablespoon Earthrise® Spirulina
- 1 teaspoon of Fresh Lemon Juice
- 1 Dash Garlic Powder
- 1 Dash Salt
- 1 Dash Pepper

- Combine all of the ingredients

* Healthy Options: Mix a small amount of wasabi paste to give the dressing some spiciness

This dressing offers two (2) servings.

WILD GREEN DRESSING

- 1 teaspoon Earthrise® Spirulina
- 4 Tablespoons Mayonnaise
- 2 Tablespoons Shoyu
- 1/8 teaspoon Wasabi Paste

- Mix well in the bowl with fork and pour over your greens

This dressing offers two (2) servings.

FISH SALAD NATURAL

- 3 Fresh Green Onions
- 2 Medium Avocados
- 2 Stalks of Fresh Celery
- 1 Can of Salmon
- 1 Tablespoon of Fresh Coriander, Minced
- 1 Tablespoon of Shoyu
- 1 Tablespoon Earthrise® Spirulina
- 2 teaspoons of Chili Sauce
- 1/2 teaspoon of Freshly Ground Ginger

- In a mixing bowl, mix all of the ingredients except the avocado
- Cover the bowl and place in the refrigerator for 2 – 3 hours
- Peel & pit the avocados, then slice thinly
- Divide the mixture into four bowls and arrange the avocado slices around each bowl

* Healthy Options: Sprinkle some freshly grated parmesan cheese over each salad.

This salad serves four (4) servings.

CABBAGE SALAD

- 3 Eggs (Separate eggs & yolks)
- 1/2 Head of Green Cabbage
- 1/3 Cup Rice Vinegar
- 1/3 Cup of Heavy Cream
- 1/3 Cup Warm Water
- 1 Tablespoon of Clover Honey
- 1 Tablespoon of Butter
- 1 Tablespoon of Earthrise® Spirulina
- 1 teaspoon of Dry Mustard
- 1 teaspoon of Freshly Ground Black Pepper
- 1/2 teaspoon of Salt
- 1/2 teaspoon of Paprika

- Combine the egg yolks, rice vinegar, heavy cream, water, butter, honey and mustard into a medium saucepan
- Cook over a low heat until the mixture becomes thick
- Add the remaining ingredients (except egg whites), pour into a serving bowl and refrigerate
- Cook the egg whites until firm, chop finely and place in the refrigerator
- Clean the cabbage
- Place on a chopping board and carefully chop into thin slices
- Just prior to serving, mix the egg whites into the dressing

* Healthy Options: Sprinkle some herbed croutons onto each salad

This salad offers four (4) servings.

SESAME SALAD WITH DRESSING

- 1 Egg Yolk
- 1 Clove of Garlic, Crushed
- 1/2 Head of Green Cabbage
- 1/4 Cup of Olive Oil
- 2 Tablespoons of Shoyu
- 2 Tablespoons of Sesame Oil
- 2 Tablespoons of Fresh White Sesame Seeds
- 1 Tablespoon of Dijon Style Mustard
- 1 Tablespoon of Rice Vinegar
- 1 Tablespoon of Earthrise® Spirulina
- 1 teaspoon of Lemon Juice
- 1/2 teaspoon of Sea Salt
- 1/2 teaspoon of Freshly Ground Black Pepper

- Combine the mustard, vinegar, Shoyu, egg yolk, garlic cloves and Earthrise® Spirulina in a medium mixing bowl
- Next, add the olive oil & sesame oil, whisking while pouring the two oils into the mixture
- Stir in the lemon juice, salt, pepper and sesame seeds
- Toss your favorite greens with this unique dressing

* Healthy Options: Mix a small amount of wasabi paste to give the dressing some spiciness

This dressing offers four (4) servings.

SESAME SPINACH SALAD

- 4 Water Chestnuts, Thinly Sliced
- 2 Large Mushrooms, thinly sliced
- 1/2 Pound Fresh Spinach
- 1/4 Sweet Red Onion, Thinly Sliced
- 3 Tablespoons of Virgin Olive Oil
- 2 Tablespoons White Toasted Sesame Seeds
- 1 Tablespoon Earthrise® Spirulina
- 1 teaspoon Fresh Lemon Juice
- 1 teaspoon Tamari
- 1 Dash of Salt
- 1 Dash of Pepper

- Remove the stems from the spinach, wash and drain
- Whisk the oil, lemon juice, tamari, salt, pepper and Spirulina together
- Next, mix in the chestnuts and mushrooms
- Cover and refrigerate for at least one hour
- Cut the spinach into easy to eat pieces and put in a medium mixing bowl
- Pour in the dressing and toss well

* Healthy Options: Mix a small amount of anchovies into the salad

This dressing offers four (4) servings.

CITUS YOGURT DRESSING

- 1 Cup of Plain Yogurt
- 3 Tablespoons of Freshly Squeezed Orange Juice
- 2 Tablespoons of Honey
- 2 Tablespoon of Freshly Squeezed Lemon Juice
- 1 Tablespoon of Fresh Mint, Finely Chopped
- 1/2 Tablespoon of Earthrise® Spirulina

- Combine all of the ingredients (except Earthrise® Spirulina) in a medium mixing bowl and mix well
- Next, carefully whisk the Earthrise® Spirulina into the mixture

* Healthy Options: Use grapefruit juice in place of the orange juice for a tangier taste

This dressing offers four to five (4-5) servings.

SIMPLE RED DRESSING

- 1 Cup Olive Oil
- 1/3 Cup Rice Vinegar
- 3 Tablespoons of Tomato Sauce
- 1-1/2 Tablespoons Earthrise® Spirulina
- 1 Tablespoon of Shoyu
- 1 teaspoon of Dry Mustard
- 1 teaspoon of Honey
- 1/4 teaspoon Freshly Chopped Oregano
- 1 Dash of Salt

- Mix all of the ingredients together well in a small mixing bowl
- Serve Chilled

* Healthy Options: Substitute Fresh thyme for the oregano

This dressing offers four (4) servings.

SIMPLE GREEN DRESSING

- 1 Cup Olive Oil
- 1/3 Cup Rice Vinegar
- 2 Tablespoons Earthrise® Spirulina

- Mix all of the ingredients together well in a small mixing bowl
- Serve Chilled

* Healthy Options: Mix some chopped fresh basil for a tangy taste

This dressing offers four (4) servings.

SOUPS

Earthrise® Spirulina increases antioxidant protection.*

* These statements have not been evaluated by the Food and Drug Administration. This product is not intended to diagnose, treat, cure or prevent disease.

SPIRA-ZUCCHINI SOUP

- 6 Cups of Fresh Zucchini, Diced
- 6 Cups of Vegetable Stock
- 2 Celery Stalks, Finely Chopped
- 1 Pound of Fresh Spinach or your favorite Green Vegetable
  1 Bay Leaf
- 1/2 Onion (White or Yellow), Finely Chopped
- 3/4 Cups of Split Green Peas (Drained and Rinsed)
- 1/4 Cup Fresh Parsley, Chopped Finely
- 2 Tablespoons of Virgin Olive Oil
- 2 Tablespoon of Earthrise® Spirulina
- 1/4 teaspoon of Fresh Basil
- 1 Dash of Salt to Taste

- Combine the oil, the onion and the celery in a large pot.
- Sauté until the two vegetables are very soft
- Add 4 cups of the vegetable stock into the pot, along with the peas and the bay leaf
- Bring the mixture to a boil and then simmer on a low heat for 45 minutes
- Add the zucchini, the remaining vegetable stock and the seasonings into the mixture
- Continue cooking the mixture for another 10 minutes
- Remove the bay leaf and discard it
- Pour the mixture into the blender and purée until smooth
- Pour the mixture back into the pot and then add the spinach (or other green vegetable) as well as the parsley
- Cook the mixture over a medium heat for five minutes
- Remove the pot from the stove
- Quickly whisk the Spirulina into the mixture

* Healthy Options: Serve with herbed croutons or sprinkle some parmesan cheese on top of each bowl of soup.

This soup offers seven to eight (7 - 8) bowls.

COOL SPIRULINA SOUP

- 11 Ounces of Vegetable Stock
- 3 Medium Tomatoes
- 2 Medium Avocados
- 1 Green Onion, Finely Chopped
- 1/2 Cup of Sour Cream
- 1 Tablespoon of Lemon Juice
- 1 Tablespoon of Earthrise® Spirulina
- 1 teaspoon of Salt
- 1/2 teaspoon of Curry Powder
- 1 Dash of Hot Pepper (Optional)

- Peel and dice the avocados
- Chop the tomatoes into small pieces
- Combine all of the ingredients, except the tomato, into the blender and blend on high for 3 – 5 minutes
- Pour into a large serving bowl
- Mix the tomato's into the soup
- Chill for approximately one hour
- When serving, garnish with a tablespoon of sour cream and chopped green onions with a dash of pepper

* Healthy Options: Serve with herbed croutons on top of each bowl of soup.

This soup offers five to six (5 - 6) bowls.

SPEEDY SPIRULINA SOUP

- 4 Cups of Tomato Juice
- 1/2 Cup of Dried Onion
- 1 Tablespoon of Earthrise® Spirulina
- 1 Dash of Salt (to Taste)
- 1 Dash of Pepper (to Taste)
- 1 Dash of Hot Sauce (Optional)

- Combine all of the ingredients into a medium pot
- Cook on a medium heat until just before boiling

* Healthy Options: Serve with herbed croutons on top of each bowl of soup.

This soup offers four (4) bowls.

MISO SPIRULINA SOUP

- 1-½ Cups of Warm Water
- 1 Heaping Tablespoon of Miso Paste
- 1 Tablespoon of Earthrise® Spirulina
- 1 teaspoon of Nutritional Yeast

- Combine all of the ingredients into a blender and blend well
- Pour into a small saucepan and heat over a low heat until just before boiling

* Healthy Options: Cook with some chopped parsley

This soup offers one (1) bowl.

CREAM OF BROCCOLI SOUP

- 1-1/2 to 2 Pounds of Broccoli
- 4 Cups of Milk (Vegetable Stock may be Substituted)
- 2 Tablespoons of Butter
- 2 Tablespoons of Flour
- 1 Tablespoon of Earthrise® Spirulina
- 1 teaspoon of Salt
- 1 Dash of Pepper

- Rinse the broccoli, trim the flowerets and discard the thick stems (do not put down your garbage disposal)
- Place the flowerets into a large pot of boiling water and cook uncovered until tender.
- Place the milk into a small saucepan and cook on a high heat until scalded
- Slowly feed the flowerets into a blender with the milk until puréed (set aside six small pieces for garnish)
- Melt the butter in a large saucepan
- Add the flour, using a fork to mix it into the butter
- Add the salt and pepper into the butter mixture
- Pour the broccoli purée mixture into the saucepan
- Bring the stove up to a medium heat and bring to a boil, stirring constantly
- Quickly whisk in the Spirulina
- Garnish the bowls with the remaining flowerets that were set aside earlier

* Healthy Options: Sprinkle some Pepitas (Pumpkin Seeds) on top of each bowl of soup for contrasting color.

This soup offers five to six (5 - 6) bowls.

COLD BROCCOLI SOUP

- 1-1/2 to 2 Pounds of Broccoli
- 1 Large Onion, Finely Chopped
- 1 Clove of Garlic
- 4 Cups Vegetable Stock (Chicken Stock may be substituted)
- 1 Cup of Light Cream (Half & Half)
- 3/4 Cup Celery, Finely Chopped
- 1-1/2 Tablespoons of Earthrise® Spirulina
- 1 Tablespoon of Fresh Lemon Juice
- 1 Tablespoon of Cornstarch
- 1/2 teaspoon of Black Pepper
- 1 Dash of Salt

- Rinse the broccoli and trim the flowerets and discard the thick stems (do not put down your garbage disposal)
- Place the flowerets into a large pot with the stock and cook uncovered on a high heat until the stock starts to boil
- Reduce the heat and simmer on a low heat until the broccoli is tender
- Add all of the remaining ingredients except the Spirulina and the cream and mix well
- Set aside to cool off
- Add the Spirulina and whisk very well to avoid it from forming lumps in the mixture
- Place the pot into the refrigerator to chill for at least an hour before serving
- Just before serving, gently stir the cream into the mixture
- After pouring the mixture into the bowls, place a broccoli floweret in the middle of each bowl

* Healthy Options: Sprinkle some Herbed Croutons on top of each bowl of soup.

This soup offers seven to eight (7 - 8) bowls.

FRAGRANT BASIL SPIRULINA SOUP

- 2 Cloves of Garlic
- 1 Medium Egg
- 7 Cups of Chicken Broth
- 2 Cups of Fresh Spinach, Firmly Packed
- 2 Cups of Fresh Shredded Parmesan Cheese
- 1 Cup of Fresh Parsley, Firmly Packed
- 1 Cup of Orzo
- 3/4 Cup Fresh Basil Leaves, Firmly Packed
- 1/2 Cup of Warm Water
- 1/4 Cup of Walnuts (Pieces)
- 1/4 Cup of Virgin Olive Oil
- 1 Tablespoon of Earthrise® Spirulina

- Combine the spinach, parsley and 1 cup of the chicken broth into the blender
- Blend until the greens are smooth
- Add the basil, garlic, olive oil and walnuts into the blender
- Blend until the mixture is once again smooth
- Pout the mixture into a large saucepan along with the remaining stock
- Heat the mixture over a medium heat until boiling
- Add the orzo to the saucepan
- Continue heating the mixture until it returns to a boil
- Reduce the heat to simmer and cook, covered, until the orzo is tender (approximately 10 – 15 minutes)
- Beat the egg and the water in a mixing bowl
- Mix 1 cup of the parmesan cheese into the egg mixture
- Next, whip the Spirulina into the mixture
- Pour one cup of the soup mixture into the egg mixture and quickly mix together
- Pour the egg mixture into the soup pot and mix together
- Cook for a few minutes more
- Divide the soup into serving bowls and sprinkle the remaining cheese over each bowl

* Healthy Options: Substitute Sorrel, Swiss Chard or your favorite greens in place of the spinach.

This soup offers seven to eight (7 - 8) bowls.

SPIRULINA CHICKEN SOUP

- 6 Cups of Chicken Broth
- 4 Eggs
- 1 Eight (8) Ounce Package of your Favorite Noodle
- Meatballs (ground chicken, bread crumbs, an egg and a dash of salt and pepper)
- 1/2 Package of Firm Tofu
- 1 Tablespoon of Earthrise® Spirulina

- Bring the broth to a boil in a medium pot
- Add the noodles and simmer over a low heat until tender
- Beat the eggs slightly and slowly stir into the soup mixture
- Add the Meatballs and Tofu
- Quickly whisk in the Spirulina and serve

* Healthy Options: Sprinkle some chopped parsley on top of each bowl of soup.

This soup offers five to six (5-6) bowls.

SOUPED UP SPIRULINA-TOMATO SOUP

- 12 Small Sweet Red Onions, Finely Sliced
- 6 Black Peppercorns
- 5 – 6 Medium Tomatoes (Cubed)
- 4 Cloves of Garlic
- 2 Bay Leaves
- 1 White Onion (Chopped)
- 1 Piece of Cinnamon (About 1" Long)
- 4 Cups of Warm Water
- ¼ Cup of Split Peas
- ¼ Cup of Lemon Juice
- 2 Tablespoons of Vegetable Oil
- 2 Tablespoons of Earthrise® Spirulina
- 1 Dash of Salt

- Place the split peas into a medium pan of boiling water
- Add half of the oil and boil until the split peas are soft
- Mash the peas and then strain the liquid from the mixture
- Put the pea mixture into a medium pot and add the red onions, garlic, peppercorns, tomatoes and the cinnamon
- Bring the mixture to a boil
- Using a potato masher, mash the mixture until the tomatoes are completely mashed
- Mix together and bring to a boil again
- Strain the liquid into a serving bowl and add the lemon juice and the salt
- In a large pan, heat the remainder of the oil
- Add the white onion and fry until golden brown (caramelizing the onions)
- Add the bay leaves and the soup mixture
- Remove the pan from the heat and let stand 10 minutes
- Add the Spirulina and whisk well

* Healthy Options: Sprinkle some herbed croutons on top of each bowl of soup.

This soup offers four (4) bowls.

SUPER GREEN SPIRULINA SOUP

- 6 Carrots, Diced
- 6 Vegetable Broth Cubes
- 6 Garlic Cloves
- 2 White Onions, Cut in Half and Sliced Thin
- 2 Bunches of Green Onion, Diced
- 3 Quarts of Warm Water
- 4 Cups of Fresh Peas (Can Substitute Frozen)
- 1 Cup of Fresh Parsley, Chopped
- 1/3 Cup of Virgin Olive Oil
- 1/3 Cup of Brewers Yeast or Nutritional Yeast
- 1/2 Cup of Tahini
- 1/4 Cup of Earthrise® Spirulina
- 1/4 Cup of Dark Miso Paste
- 2 teaspoons of Salt

- Put all except 2 cups of the water into a large pot, along with the salt and heat on high until it starts to boil
- Sauté the white onions, carrots and green onions in the oil until the while onions become transparent
- Add to the water and simmer on a low heat until the carrots are tender
- During the time that this mixture is simmering, put the remaining water, the yeast, vegetable broth powder, tahini, garlic, miso and the cayenne pepper into a blender and blend in high until completely smooth
- Turn the blender on the lowest mix setting and add the Spirulina
- Once the carrots of tender, add the parsley and peas to the soup mixture and cook for an additional five minutes
- Pour the mixture from the blender into the soup and mix well – being careful to NOT bring the soup mixture to a boil

* Healthy Options: Sprinkle some chopped parsley on top of each bowl of soup.

This soup offers ten (10) bowls.

SPIRULINA SPRINGTIME SOUP

- 6 Cups of Chicken Broth
- 1 Pound of Fresh Spinach (Stems Removed)
- 1 Medium Bunch of Watercress (Stems Removed)
- 1 Cup of Cooked Green Peas
- 1/2 Cup of Sour Cream
- 1/4 Cup of Butter
- 1/4 Cup Of Flour
- 1 Tablespoon of Earthrise® Spirulina
- 1 Tablespoon of Fresh Chives (Diced)

- Pour the chicken broth in to a large pot and cook over a medium heat until it come to a boil
- Add the spinach and watercress, then continue cooking until it starts to boil again
- Reduce the heat and simmer for five minutes
- Move the pot off of the stove to allow it to cool down for about fifteen minutes
- Once cooled, pour part of the mixture into the blender and purée
- Next, purée the rest of the mixture
- In the empty pot, melt the butter over a medium heat
- Quickly stir in the flour, mixing it well with the butter, cooking it until it starts to turn brown (a minute or two should be enough)
- Add the puréed mixture back to the pot, stirring it constantly until it thickens
- Quickly whisk in the Spirulina
- Stir in the peas
- Simmer on the lowest possible heat and do NOT bring to a boil
- Combine the sour cream and the chives in a small bowl
- Top each bowl of soup with a dollop of the sour cream mixture

* Healthy Options: Use a low fat sour cream.

This soup offers seven to eight (5-6) bowls.

SIDE DISHES

Earthrise® Spirulina contains a variety of carotenoids, which work in synergy as antioxidants protecting our cells from the damaging effects of free-radicals. The two most important carotenoids are 1) beta-carotene (known to promote cellular health) and 2) zeaxanthin (known to promote eye health).*

* These statements have not been evaluated by the Food and Drug Administration. This product is not intended to diagnose, treat, cure or prevent disease.

NUTTY SPIRULINA RICE

- 2 Large White Onions, Coarsely Chopped
- 1 Medium Egg
- Sliced Almonds
- Coconut Flakes
- 4 Ounces of Crushed or Ground Walnuts
- 1 Cup of Brown Rice
- 2 Tablespoon of Tomato Purée
- 1 Tablespoon of Fresh Chopped Sage
- 1 Tablespoon of Fresh Chopped Parsley
- 1 Tablespoon of Fresh Chopped Celery
- 1-½ Tablespoons of Earthrise® Spirulina
- 1 Dash of Salt
- 1 Dash of Pepper

- Cook the rice in your usual manner (under tender and not mushy)
- In a saucepan, sauté the onions until soft
- Add the tomato purée to the onions and heat up
- Add the sage, parsley, celery, salt and pepper to the mixture and mix well
- Combine the onion mixture to the finished rice in a medium pot
- Add the Spirulina to the entire mixture
- Place the mixture into a serving bowl and ring the edges with the almond slices while sprinkling the coconut flakes around the middle of the dish

* Healthy Options: Sprinkle some chopped parsley on top of the serving bowl.

This side dish offers four to (4 - 5) servings.

GLORIOUS GREEN MOUSSE

- 2 Large Ripe Avocados
- 2 Ripe Cucumbers
- 1/2 Cup of Virgin Olive Oil
- 1/4 Cup of Fresh Lemon Juice
- 3 Tablespoons of Heavy Cream
- 3 Tablespoons of Mayonnaise
- 1 Tablespoon of Earthrise® Spirulina
- 1 Dash Salt
- 1 Dash Pepper

- Peel and pit the avocados, then slice into slices
- Combine the olive oil, lemon juice, salt and pepper together
- Put the oil mixture, with the avocados, into the blender and purée until smooth
- In a mixing bowl, combine the cream, mayonnaise and Spirulina and whip until light and fluffy
- Combine the oil mixture and the avocado mixture
- Peel the cucumber and slice thickly
- Pour the mousse into 6 shallow bowls and garnish with the cucumber slices

* Healthy Options: Substitute you favorite sliced vegetables.

This side dish offers six (6) servings.

ICED CORNBREAD

- Cornbread
  - 1 Egg
  - 2 Cups Yellow (or Blue) Cornmeal
  - 1 Cup Fresh Corn Kernels (Uncooked)
  - 1 Cup Milk
  - 3 Tablespoons Butter (Melted)
  - 1 Tablespoon Maple Syrup
  - 2-1/2 teaspoons Baking Powder
  - 1/4 teaspoon Salt
- Icing
  - 3 Scallions, Chopped
  - 1 Garlic Clove, Finely Chopped
  - 6 Ounces Soft Cream Cheese
  - 2 Tablespoons Sour Cream
  - 1 teaspoon Earthrise® Spirulina

- Preheat over to 425
- Butter a baking pan (9" x 9")
- In a large mixing bowl, combine the baking powder, salt and cornmeal
- In another mixing bowl, beat the egg
- Add the melted butter, milk and maple syrup
- Combine both mixtures into one bowl
- Add the corn, only mixing for a few moments (do not over-mix)
- Pour the mixture into the buttered pan
- Bake for approximately 20 – 25 minutes
- Remove from the pan and let cool
- To mix the icing, mix the cream cheese (room temperature) and the sour cream in a small mixing bowl
- Once smooth, add the Spirulina and then mix in the scallions and garlic
- Use the icing on the cornbread once it's cooled

This side dish offers twelve (12) servings.

GARDEN STUFFED POTATOES

- 4 Large Baking Potatoes
- 2 Medium White Onions, Diced
- 1/2 Cup Corn, Cooked
- 1/2Cup Fresh Celery, Diced
- 1/2 Cup Frozen Baby Peas
- 1/2 Cup Plain Yogurt
- 1/4 Cup Warm Water
- 2 Tablespoons Fresh Sweet Basil, Chopped
- 2 Tablespoons Brewers Yeast
- 1 Tablespoon Earthrise® Spirulina
- 2 teaspoons Tamari
- 2 teaspoons Oregano
- 1 teaspoon Fresh Ginger, Grated
- 1/2 teaspoon Chili Powder

- Preheat the oven to 400°
- Cook the potatoes in the microwave
- Carefully slice the potatoes in half, then scoop out all but a thin layer of the potato
- Sauté all of the other ingredients (except the Spirulina and yogurt)
- Mix the scooped potato into the sauté mixture
- Mix the Spirulina and yogurt into the potato mixture
- Add salt and pepper to taste
- Spoon the potato mixture back into the potato shells
- Place the filled shells onto an oiled cookie sheet
- Bake for 15 minutes

* Healthy Options: Sprinkle some chopped chives onto each potato.

This side dish offers four (4) servings

TINTED MASHED POTATOES

- 6 Medium Baking Potatoes
- 1/2 Cup Milk
- 2 Tablespoons Butter
- 1 Tablespoon Parsley, Chopped
- 1 teaspoon Earthrise® Spirulina
- 1 Dash Salt
- 1 Dash Pepper

- Peel, cube and boil the potatoes until soft
- In a large mixing bowl, mash them well
- Mix in the milk and butter until smooth
- Add the Spirulina, salt and pepper, then mix well
- Sprinkle the chopped parsley then serve

* Healthy Options: Sprinkle some chopped chives onto each potato.

This side dish offers six (6) servings

DILLED GREEN BEANS

- 1 Medium Lemon, Juiced
- 1/2 Pound Green Beans
- 1 Medium Red Onion, Thinly Sliced
- 1 Fresh Garlic Clove, Sliced
- 1/2 Cup Slivered Almonds
- 1/4 Cup Fresh Dill, Finely Chopped
- 1 teaspoon, Virgin Oil
- 1 teaspoon Earthrise® Spirulina
- 1 Dash Salt
- 1 Dash Pepper

- Wash and steam the green beans, onions and garlic for 5 minutes
- Pour off any excess water
- Drizzle the olive oil over the vegetables and toss well
- Add all of the remaining ingredients except the Spirulina and toss well
- Sprinkle the Spirulina and toss again

* Healthy Options: Add some finely slivered carrots for color.

This side dish offers four (4) servings.

FISH ROLLERS

- Sauce
  - 3 Tablespoons of Melted Butter
  - 2 Tablespoons of Shoyu (Soy Sauce)
  - 1 tablespoon of Earthrise® Spirulina
  - 1-1/2 teaspoons of Molasses
  - 1/2 teaspoon of Ginger Powder
  - 1/2 teaspoon of Chinese Five Spices (Available in most Asian Style Grocery Stores)

- Fish
  - 6 Fillets of Sole
  - 3 Finely Chopped Green Onions
  - 1 Garlic Clove (Crushed)
  - 1/2 Pound of Crab Meat
  - 1 Tablespoon of Earthrise® Spirulina
  - 1 Tablespoon of Butter
  - 1 teaspoon of Finely Chopped Parsley
  - 1 teaspoon of Fresh lemon Juice
  - 1 Dash of Salt
  - 1 Dash of Pepper

- Preheat the oven to 350°
- Mix the sauce ingredients in a small mixing bowl
- Flatten the fish fillets by placing them in between two sheets of wax paper and pounding them with a meat tenderizer or the bottom of a heavy glass
- In a mixing bowl, mix crab meat, green onions, parsley, Spirulina, garlic, butter, salt, pepper and lemon juice
- Divide the crab mixture into six sections and roll each section into a long roll and place each roll on a flattened fish fillet
- Roll each fillet up and secure with toothpicks
- Lightly oil the bottom of an oven proof dish, arrange the six rolls on the dish and cover them with the sauce
- Bake for 30 – 45 minutes
- Slice each fillet into several sections and serve on a bed of pilaf or brown rice

* Healthy Options: Substitute a bed of green cabbage for the rice.

This side dish offers approximately six (6) servings.

SPIRULINA SPINACH BALLS

- 4 Garlic Cloves
- 1-1/2 Pounds of Fresh Spinach
- 1 Green Chili (Optional)
- 1 – 2 Tablespoons of Flour
- 1 Tablespoon of Earthrise® Spirulina
- 1/2 teaspoon of Fresh Ginger, Grated
- 1/2 teaspoon of Salt
- 1/2 teaspoon of Curry Powder

- Wash the spinach and cook in the microwave for two minutes
- Pat dry and purée in the blender
- Add all of the other ingredients except the flour and mix well
- Add enough flour to make the mixture into a paste like texture
- Heat some vegetable oil in a medium pot and heat on a medium heat
- Roll the mixture into small balls and deep fry a few minutes each
- Place on some paper towels to drain excess oil
- Serve with your favorite curry sauce

* Healthy Options: Serve with a low calorie blue cheese dressing for a tangy taste.

This side dish serves four (4) people.

PILAF SPIRULINA

- 10 Medium Button Mushrooms, sliced and quartered
- 2 Medium Tomatoes, Diced
- 1 Red Bell Pepper, Cut into Strips
- 1 Fresh Small Onion, Finely Chopped
- 1/2 Pound of Sharp Cheddar Cheese, Coarsely Grated
- 1/2 Stick of Butter
- 2 Cups of Kasha
- 2 Cups of Chicken Broth
- 1 Cup of Fresh Green Peas, Cooked
- 1 Cup of Fresh Celery, Finely Chopped
- 1-1/2 Tablespoon of Earthrise® Spirulina
- 1 Tablespoon of Chili Powder
- 1 teaspoon of Salt & Pepper to Taste
- 1/2 teaspoon of Fresh Oregano, Finely Chopped

- Preheat the oven to 350°
- Heat the chicken stock over a medium flame
- Once boiling, cook the kasha until the fluid is absorbed
- Combine the kasha in a mixing bowl with the tomatoes, green peas, chili powder, salt and pepper.
- In a medium skillet, sauté the celery, mushrooms and onion in the butter over a high heat until they are soft
- Combine the vegetables with the kasha mixture, then add the oregano and any other seasonings that you like
- Butter a gratin (rectangular) dish, pour the mixture into the dish, cover and bake for 30 minutes
- Once you remove the dish from the oven, sprinkle the Spirulina over the mixture and then the grated cheese
- Garnish the dish with the bell paper

* Healthy Options: Substitute freshly grated parmesan cheese for the cheddar cheese.

This side dish serves six (6) people.

NUTTY POTATO BAKE

- Potato Cake
  - 3 Medium Baking Potatoes
  - 1 Red Bell Pepper
  - 1/2 Pound of Unsalted Sunflower Seed
  - 1/4 Pound of Butter
  - 1 Cup of Ground Pecans
  - 1 Cup of Fresh Celery, Chopped
  - 1 Cup of Fresh Carrots, Grated
  - 1 Cup of White Onion, Grated
  - 1/4 Cup of Fresh Parsley, Chopped
  - 1/4 Cup of Earthrise® Spirulina
  - 3 Tablespoons of Nutritional Yeast
  - 1 Tablespoon of Fresh Chives, Chopped
  - 1 teaspoon of Salt
  - 1 teaspoon of Fresh Thyme
  - 1/4 teaspoon of Grated Nutmeg
  - 1/4 teaspoon of Freshly Grated Black Pepper
- Peanut Sauce
  - 1-1/2 Sticks of Butter
  - 3/4 Cup of Unsalted Peanuts, Crushed
  - 1/4 Cup of Fresh Parsley, Finely Chopped
  - 1/8 Cup of Shallots, Minced

- Preheat the oven to 350°
- Sauté the onion in some butter
- Put all of the ingredients, except the bell pepper, into a blender and blend until all of the ingredients are combined
- Pour the mixture into an oiled baking pan
- Bake approximately 45 minutes
- Slice the bell pepper and use it to garnish the dish and the nut sauce
- To make the sauce, melt the butter in a large saucepan and add the peanuts
- Cook over a low heat until the peanuts start to turn brown
- Add the parsley and shallots, mix well
- Pour over the Potato Bake

* Healthy Options: Substitute other nuts for the peanuts in the sauce mix

This side dish serves six (6) people.

CREAMED SPIRULINA SPINACH

- 3 Pounds of Fresh Spinach
- 6 Tablespoons of Butter
- 2 Cups of Heavy Cream
- 1 Tablespoon of Earthrise® Spirulina
- 1/4 teaspoon of Grated Nutmeg

- Wash the spinach and trim off the ends of the stems
- Place into a large pot and cook until the spinach is tender (use only the water that is on the spinach after washing it)
- Move the spinach to a colander and squeeze as much water as possible out of it
- Finely chop the spinach
- Combine the spinach and the butter in a large saucepan and cook over a medium heat until the moisture is gone
- Add the cream, a little as a time, stirring the entire time
- Sprinkle the nutmeg, salt and the pepper over the spinach mixture
- Simmer over a low heat until the cream is reduced
- Remove the pan from the stove
- Mix the Earthrise® Spirulina into the mixture
- Move the mixture to a nice serving dish

* Healthy Options: Add some sliced almonds or some herbed croutons to the edges of the dish

This side dish serves six (6) people.

VEGETARIAN DISHES

Earthrise® Spirulina promotes longevity.*

* These statements have not been evaluated by the Food and Drug Administration.
This product is not intended to diagnose, treat, cure or prevent disease.

VEGETARIAN LOAF WITH SPIRULINA MUSHROOM SAUCE

- Vegetarian Loaf
    - 2 Pounds of Fresh Spinach (with the Stems Removed)
    - 4 Medium Eggs
    - 1 Cup of Half and Half
    - 2/3 Cup of Dry Bread Crumbs
    - 1/2 Cup of Chopped Green Onion
    - 1/2 Cup of Grated Parmesan Cheese
    - 3 Tablespoons of Butter
    - 3 Tablespoons of Sesame Seeds
    - 1 teaspoon of Salt
    - 1/2 teaspoon of Nutmeg
    - 1/2 teaspoon of Pepper
- Sauce
    - 1 Cup of Fresh Button Mushrooms, Sliced Thin
    - 1 Cup of Half and Half
    - 6 Tablespoons of Butter
    - 3 Tablespoons of Flour
    - 1 Tablespoon of Earthrise® Spirulina
    - 1 Dash of Salt
    - 1 Dash of Pepper

- Preheat the oven to 350°
- Wash the spinach and steam it in the microwave for 2 minutes
- Quickly cool it off in cold water and squeeze the excess water off of it
- Chop it finely and set aside
- Using a small saucepan, sauté the onion in butter until soft
- Combine the eggs, half and half and the other seasonings in a large bowl
- Add the spinach into the large bowl and mix well
- Next, add the onion, bread crumbs, cheese and the sesame seeds
- Spoon the spinach mixture into a greased loaf type pan or a ring type mold
- Place the pan in a shallow baking pan and put some water in this pan
- Put both of the pans into the oven and bake approximately 1 hour (you should be able to out a knife into the loaf and have it come out clean)

- Remove the inner pan from the water and let it stand 10 minutes
- Put the mold upside down so that the loaf comes out onto a serving platter
- Sauté the mushrooms in 3 Tablespoons of the butter in a small skillet over medium heat until they are tender
- Melt the remaining butter in a medium saucepan over a medium heat
- Stir in the flour, salt and pepper and mix well
- Cook and stir until the flour starts to brown
- Slowly add the half and half, whisking so there are no lumps and the mixture gets thicker
- Whisk in the Spirulina Stir in the mushrooms
- Drizzle some of the Earthrise® Spirulina Mushroom Sauce over the top pf the load and serve the rest in a small serving bowl

* Healthy Options: Serve with The Green Mousse.

This dish serves eight (8) people.

VEGETABLE SPIRULINA STIR-FRY

- 8 Large Carrots
- 4 Medium Zucchinis
- 2 Large White Onions
- 2 Green Cabbages
- 1 Cup of Sesame Oil
- 6 Tablespoons of Shoyu
- 1-½ Tablespoons of Earthrise® Spirulina

- Chop all of the vegetables (separately)
- Heat the oil in a large frying pan on the highest temperature
- Add the zucchini, onions and carrots
- Stir well and fry for 2 minutes
- Add the cabbage to the mixture
- Fry for another 2 minutes
- Add the Shoyu and mix
- Remove the pan from the heat and cover for one minute
- Add the Spirulina and mix well

* Healthy Options: Add some chopped chili peppers for some spice

This side dish serves six (6) people.

CURRY EGGPLANT AND POTATOES

- 4 Fresh Garlic Cloves, Crushed
- 4 Medium Tomatoes, Cut into Wedges
- 3 Large Baking Potatoes
- 2 Medium Italian Eggplants (or 4 Japanese Eggplants)
- 2 Green Bell Peppers
- 1-1/2 Cups Warm Water
- 3 Tablespoons, Virgin Olive Oil
- 1 Tablespoon Earthrise® Spirulina
- 1-1/2 teaspoons Salt
- 1 teaspoon of Fresh Ginger, Grated
- 1 teaspoon Red Mustard Seeds
- 1 teaspoon Turmeric
- 1 teaspoon Cumin Seeds
- 1/2 teaspoon Cayenne Pepper
- 1/2 teaspoon Fresh Coriander, Ground
- 1/2 teaspoon Cinnamon
- 1/2 teaspoon ground Black Pepper

- Wash the eggplant and cut into 1" thick slices
- Place into a mixing bowl, sprinkle salt over the slices and set aside for 30 minutes
- Squeeze out all of the water from the eggplant slices, then cut the slices into cubes
- Peel and cube the potatoes
- Cut the bell pepper into ½" squares
- Heat the olive oil in a large frying pan
- Add all of the spices and the garlic, sautéing for a few minutes
- Add the eggplant, potatoes and peppers
- Toss everything until well coated with the oil mixture
- Add the water, cover the pan and simmer for 20 – 25 minutes, stirring occasionally
- Remove the cover and cook over a low heat for another 15 minutes, stirring gently
- Add the tomatoes, cooking for a few minutes more until they are warm
- Pour the mixture into a serving bowl and sprinkle the Spirulina over it

* Healthy Options: Substitute 6–8 red potatoes for the baking potatoes.

This side dish offers six (6) servings.

MAIN DISHES

Eat your SPIRULINA greens for good health!* Supplement your intake of fruits and vegetables with 1 serving of Earthrise® Spirulina a day for the equivalent to 3 – 4 servings of common vegetables a day in terms of antioxidant content.*

* These statements have not been evaluated by the Food and Drug Administration. This product is not intended to diagnose, treat, cure or prevent disease.

SPIRULINA CREPES

- Crêpes
    - 2 Eggs
    - 1 Cup of Warm Water
    - 1 Cup of Flour
    - 1/2 Cup of Milk
    - 2 Tablespoons of Oil
    - 1 Dash of Salt
- Filling
    - 10 Ounces of Fresh Spinach
    - 1/2 Cup of Whipping Cream
    - 1/2 Cup of Shredded Swiss Cheese
    - 1/4 Cup of Grated Parmesan Cheese
    - 2 Tablespoon of Butter
    - 2 Tablespoons of Flour
    - 2 Tablespoons of Parsley Springs (Finely Chopped)
    - 1 Tablespoon of Earthrise® Spirulina
    - 1/2 teaspoon of Salt
    - 1/2 teaspoon of Nutmeg
    - 1/2 teaspoon of Ground Pepper

- Starting with the crêpes, blend the water, milk eggs, flour, oil and salt in a blender until the mixture is smooth
- Cover and refrigerate for 2 hours
- Heat a lightly oiled crêpe pan or shallow frying pan over a medium heat
- Spoon 3 tablespoons of the chilled batter onto the heated pan
- Quickly tilt the pan around until the bottom of the pan is evenly coated
- Cook until the batter is light brown on both sides of the crêpe (1-½ to 2 minutes per side)
- Cook all of the crêpes
- Preheat the oven to 350°
- To start the filling, cook the spinach in the microwave for 2 minutes
- Rinse in cold water
- Squeeze out the excess water
- Chop finely
- In a medium saucepan, melt the butter over a medium heat
- Stir in the flour, salt, nutmeg and the pepper
- Mix well and cook for 2 minutes

- Slowly stir in the cream
- Stir constantly until the mixture thickens
- Stir in the chopped spinach, the Swiss cheese and the Spirulina
- Spoon approximately 1 Tablespoon of the spinach mixture onto the center of each crêpe and roll up
- Arrange the rolled crêpes in a single layer in a baking dish
- Bake the crêpes until warm, 5 to 10 minutes
- Sprinkle the parmesan cheese on the crêpes

* Healthy Options: Garnish with parsley sprigs and serve with a natural fruit preserve or diced tomatoes

This main dish serves about one dozen (12) crêpes.

STUFFED AVOCADOS

- 8 Button Mushrooms, Sliced Thickly
- 3 Large Avocados
- 1 Green Bell Pepper, Diced
- 1 Egg Yolk, Lightly Beaten
- 1 Cup of Heavy Cream
- 1 Cup of Bay Shrimp
- 1 Dash of Salt
- 1 Dash of Pepper
- 2 Tablespoons of Earthrise® Spirulina
- 1 Tablespoon of Butter
- 1 Tablespoon of Lemon Juice

- Preheat the oven on the broiler setting
- Sauté the green bell peppers in a bit of oil over a medium heat until they are soft
- Add the sliced mushrooms and cook for a minute
- Drain off the oil
- Add the cream, then bring to a boil while constantly stirring
- Set off of the heat
- Cut the avocados in half (lengthwise) and carefully remove the pits
- Scoop out the meat, being careful not to tear the shells
- Cube the avocado meat and add it to the vegetable mixture
- Cook over a medium heat until the sauce becomes thick (~10 minutes)
- Remove the pan from the stove and stir in the egg yolk, the Spirulina as well as the salt and pepper
- Mix the Shrimp into the mixture
- Add the lemon juice
- Fill the empty shells with the mixture and place them on a baking sheet
- Broil for one minute

* Healthy Options: Mixed some diced tomatoes into the mixture.

This main dish serves six (6) people.

SPIRULINA STEW

- 8 Eggs
- 4 Green Onions, Minced
- 2 Cloves of Garlic, Finely Chopped
- 1 Pound of Fresh Spinach
- 1/2 Bunch of Fresh Parsley
- 4 Cups of Ricotta Cheese
- 1 Cup of Ground Beef (Lowest Fat)
- 1-1/2 Cups of Milk
- 1/4 Cup of Earthrise® Spirulina
- 4 Tablespoons of Butter
- 1/2 teaspoon of Paprika
- 1/2 teaspoon of Grated Nutmeg
- 1/4 teaspoon of Salt
- 1/4 teaspoon of Ground Black Pepper

- Preheat the oven to 325°
- In a saucepan, sauté the ground beef, drain the fat and set the beef aside
- In the same saucepan, sauté the onions, garlic and parsley in the butter over a medium heat until the onions are soft
- Rinse the spinach, squeeze as much water from it and chop it up finely
- Sauté the mixture for 5 minutes on a medium heat
- Add the beef to the spinach mixture and cook for a few minutes
- Stir in the Spirulina & remove from the stove
- In a large mixing bowl, beat the cheese and the eggs until combined
- Add the milk and stir well
- Stir in the beef mixture
- Season with the grated nutmeg, the salt and the pepper
- Put the mixture into a buttered baking dish (3 to 4 quarts)
- Place the dish into a pan, add water to the pan (around the dish) and bake for 2 hours

This main dish serves six (6) people.

QUICHE LE SPIRULINE

- 4 Medium Eggs
- 1 Pre-Baked Pie Shell
- 1-1/4 Pounds of Fresh Spinach
- 1-1/2 Cups of Light Cream
- 1 Cup of Fresh Gruyere Cheese, Grated
- 2/3 Cup Grated Romano Cheese
- 3 Tablespoons of Cream Cheese
- 2 Tablespoons of Sour Cream
- 2 Tablespoons of Earthrise® Spirulina
- 2 Tablespoons of White Horseradish Sauce
- 1 Tablespoon of Worcestershire Sauce
- 1 teaspoons of Salt
- 1 teaspoon of Dried Basil Flakes
- 1 teaspoon of Ground Black Pepper
- 1/4 teaspoon of Ground Nutmeg
- 1 Dash of Tabasco Sauce

- Preheat the oven to 375°
- Wash the spinach and cook it in the microwave for 2 minutes
- Rinse in cold water to stop the cooking and squeeze the excess water out
- In a mixing bowl, combine the cream cheese, sour cream, Worcestershire, Spirulina, horseradish, salt, pepper, basil, Tabasco and nutmeg
- Add the spinach and combine well, then spread the mixture into the crust
- Whisk together 2 whole eggs along with the yolks from the other 2 eggs along with the cream
- Sprinkle the two cheeses over the spinach
- Put the pie tin onto a baking sheet
- Pour the egg mixture over the spinach
- Bake the quiche for approximately 40 minutes or until it is brown
- Cool for 10 minutes

This main dish serves six (6) people.

SPIRULINA MEATLOAF

- 18 Button Mushrooms, Chopped
- 2 Pounds of Ground Beef
- 1/4 Pound of Ham, Chopped
- 2 Eggs
- 2 Bunches of Fresh Parsley
- 2 Cloves of Garlic
- 1 Large White Onion
- 1 Red Pepper
- 1-1/2 Cups of Bread Crumbs
- 2 Tablespoons of Earthrise® Spirulina
- 2 teaspoons of Shoyu
- 1 teaspoon of Red Wine
- 1/2 teaspoon of Thyme
- 1/4 teaspoon Cayenne Pepper
- 1/4 teaspoon of Salt
- 1/4 teaspoon of Black Pepper

- Preheat the oven to 350°
- Beat the eggs
- Combine all of the ingredients in a large mixing bowl and mix very well
- Pack the mixture into a loaf shaped pan
- Bake for 1-½ hours

* Healthy Options: Garnish with sliced onions.

This main dish serves eight (8) people.

MEDITERREAN SPICY ROLLS

- 1-1/2 Pounds of Ground Lamb
- 1 Cup of Plain Yogurt
- 1 Cup of White Onion, Minced
- 1/4 Cup of Flour
- 4 Tablespoons of Butter
- 1 Tablespoon of Earthrise® Spirulina
- 1 Tablespoon of Fresh Coriander, Finely Chopped
- 1 teaspoon of Salt
- 1/2 teaspoon of Turmeric
- 1/2 teaspoon of Fresh Mint, Finely Chopped
- 1/2 teaspoon of Fresh Ground Black Pepper
- 1/4 teaspoon of Ginger

- Mix the ground lamb, onion, salt, ginger, Spirulina, turmeric, mint, coriander, pepper and half of the yogurt
- Shape into rolls, each about 6 inches long and 1 inch wide
- Melt the butter in a large frying pan
- Dip each roll into the extra yogurt and the flour
- Cook the rolls over a low heat until all sides are brown

* Healthy Options: Replace the lamb with the ground chicken.

This main dish serves four (4) people.

TURKEY DROPS

- 3 Slices of Bread, Crumbled
- 2 Cloves of Fresh Garlic, Crushed
- 2 Eggs
- 1 Pound of Turkey
- 1/4 Cup of Lime Juice
- 2 Tablespoons of White Onion, Finely Chopped
- 2 Tablespoons of Earthrise® Spirulina
- 1 teaspoon of Fennel Seeds
- 1/2 teaspoon of Ground Cinnamon
- 1/2 teaspoon of Cloves
- 1/2 teaspoon of Fresh Ground Pepper
- 1/2 teaspoon of Salt
- 1/2 teaspoon of Chili Pepper

- Fill a small pot with oil so it's about 2 inches deep and put over a medium to medium – high heat
- Combine the ground turkey, garlic, ginger, fennel seeds, cinnamon, cloves, salt, pepper and chili powder
- Next, mix the onions, bread crumbs and Spirulina into the mixture
- Beat the eggs and lime juice in a separate bowl, then mix with the meat mixture
- Form small drops with a tablespoon and carefully drop into the hot oil
- Fry each drop until brown
- Serving with your favorite dipping sauce

* Healthy Options: Replace the turkey with the ground chicken.

This main dish serves six (6) people.

DUELING TASTE FISH FILLETS

- 4 Sprigs of Fresh Parsley
- 3 Pounds of Fresh Snapper
- 2 Garlic Cloves, Minced
- 1 Large Carrot
- 1 Medium Cucumber
- 1 Sweet Pickle
- 1/2 Medium White Onion, Finely Chopped
- 1/2 of a Fresh Lemon, Sliced Thinly
- 1/2 Cup of Vinegar
- 1/2 Cup of Warm Water
- 4 Tablespoons of Virgin Olive Oil
- 2 Tablespoons of Honey
- 1-1/2 Tablespoons of Earthrise® Spirulina
- 1 Tablespoon of Corn Starch
- 1 Tablespoon of Shoyu
- 1 teaspoon of Fresh Ginger, Chopped
- 1/2 teaspoon of Salt
- 1/2 teaspoon of Ground Black Pepper

- Preheat the oven to 350°
- Prepare the cucumbers by peeling, cutting them in half, removing the seeds and then cutting into thin strips
- Peel the carrot and then cut into the same sized strips as the cucumber
- Slice the pickle into thin strips
- In a medium bowl, combine the vegetable strips with the ginger, onion, salt, pepper, honey, vinegar and water
- Allow the mixture to marinate in the refrigerator for 1 hour
- Coat the fish with some salt, pepper and your favorite seasonings
- Place the fish in a baking dish and drizzle half of the oil over the fish fillets
- Bake the fish for 20 minutes
- Drain the excess fluid from the vegetable mixture
- Mix the vegetables with the cornstarch and the Shoyu
- Pour the remaining oil into a medium frying pan and cook the garlic until brown
- Add the vegetables long enough to heat them up
- Remove from the stove and stir in the Spirulina

- Put the fish fillets onto a serving platter
- Pour the vegetables over the fish
- Arrange the parsley and lemon slices around the dish as garnish

* Healthy Options: Use orange slices in place of the lemon slices.

This main dish serves four (4) people.

DANCE OF THE SEAFOOD

- 10 – 12 Medium Cooked Shrimp
- 2 Cloves of Garlic, Minced
- 1 Can of Oysters
- 1 Large White Onion, Minced
- 1 Stick of Butter
- 1/4 Pound of Crab Meat
- 2 Cups of Chicken Broth
- 1 Cup of Long Grain Rice
- 1/2 Cup Fresh Parsley, Chopped
- 3 Tablespoons of Cooking Sherry
- 2 Tablespoons of Earthrise® Spirulina
- 1 teaspoon of Seasoned Salt
- 3/4 teaspoon of Thyme
- 1/2 teaspoon of Fennel
- 1/2 teaspoon of Ground Black Pepper

- Preheat the oven to 350°
- In a small frying pan, melt half of the butter
- Sauté the onion over a medium heat until they turn soft
- Add the rice to the onions, stirring constantly until the rice turns light brown
- Stir in the parsley, thyme garlic, fennel, seasoned salt and pepper
- Once mixed together, add the chicken broth and bring to a boil
- Transfer the mixture to a baking dish and bake for 30 minutes
- In the frying pan,.melt the rest of the butter
- Sauté the shrimp, oysters and crab for 2 minutes
- Add the sherry and stir
- Add the seafood mixture to the rice mixture, blending well
- Mix in the Spirulina and serve

* Healthy Options: Serve on a bed of lettuce or green cabbage.

This main dish serves four (4) people.

CRAB STUFFED SPINACH ROLLS

- 5 Medium Eggs
- 3 Pounds of Spinach
- 2 Cloves of Garlic, Minced
- 1 Large Carrot, Peeled and Grated
- 1/2 Small White Onion, Minced
- 1 Pound of Crab, Shredded
- 1 Cup of Bread Crumbs
- 1/2 Cup of Chives, Chopped
- 1/4 Cup of Heavy Cream
- 10 (3 extra) Tablespoons of Butter
- 2 Tablespoons of Earthrise® Spirulina
- 1 Tablespoon of Fresh Lemon Juice
- 1/2 teaspoon Cayenne Pepper
- 1/2 teaspoon of Salt
- 1/2 teaspoon of Ground Pepper
- 1/4 teaspoon of Freshly Ground Nutmeg

- Preheat the oven to 350°
- Rinse and cook the spinach in the microwave for two minutes
- Cool the spinach under cold water and squeeze as much water from it as possible
- Chop the spinach into fine pieces
- In a medium saucepan, melt 6 tablespoons of butter and then sauté the onion until slightly browned.
- Add the spinach and cook for another 3 minutes
- Slowly add the cream, stirring constantly
- Sprinkle the nutmeg, salt and pepper, mixing well
- Pour the mixture into a large mixing bowl
- Separate the yolk from the white of the eggs
- Mix the yolks into the spinach mixture
- Blend the Spirulina into the mixture
- Place a sheet of wax paper onto a buttered jellyroll pan (approximately 10" x 16") and then butter the paper
- Beat the egg whites until they are white and foamy
- Mix approximately 1/3 of the egg foam into the spinach mixture. Once blended, blend another 1/3 of the egg foam into mixture. Once blended, repeat with the final 1/3 of the egg foam
- Spread the mixture into the buttered pan
- Bake the spinach mixture for 20 minutes or until firm

- Cover the mixture with a baking cloth and a cookie sheet and turn the pan over so the mixture now sits on the cloth and cookie sheet
- Remove the waxed paper
- While the spinach mixture cools, prepare the crab stuffing
- Combine the crab meat, chives, 1 tablespoon of butter, carrots, cayenne pepper, lemon juice and garlic together
- Spread the crab stuffing carefully over the spinach mixture
- Roll the mixture into as tight of a roll as possible, wrap it in aluminum foil and place into the refrigerator for a minimum of 1 hour
- Just before serving, preheat the oven to 375°
- Unwrap the roll and slice into slices about the thickness of your thumb
- Place the slices into a well; buttered baking dish
- Melt the remaining butter in a small saucepan and mix with the breadcrumbs
- Sprinkle the breadcrumb mixture over the slices in the baking pan
- Cover the baking pan with aluminum foil
- Heat for 20 minutes

* Healthy Options: As an option, serve this dish cold on a bed of fresh lettuce leaves

This main dish serves six (6) people.

A SIMPLY GREEN CHICKEN

- 12 Button Mushrooms, Thickly Sliced
- 3 Pounds of Chicken Breasts, Cubed
- 2 Medium Sized Lemons
- 1 Pound of Fresh Spinach
- 1 Bullion Cube, Chicken Flavored
- 1/4 Pound of Unsalted Sunflower Seeds
- 3/4 Cups of Warm Water
- 1/2 Cup of Milk
- 4 Tablespoons of Butter
- 1 Tablespoon of Earthrise® Spirulina
- 1 Tablespoon of Flour
- 1 Tablespoon of Butter
- 4 teaspoons of Horseradish Sauce
- 1/2 teaspoon of Salt
- 1/4 teaspoon of Ground Black Pepper

- In a large frying pan, melt 2 tablespoons of butter over a medium heat
- Add the chicken and cooked until brown
- Add the water, the pepper and the chicken bullion cube
- Heat the mixture until it boils
- Reduce the heat to the lowest setting, cover and cook for about 30 minutes
- While the chicken is cooking, cut one of the lemons into thin slices
- Squeeze the juice out of the other lemon in preparation to be cooked
- In a large saucepan, melt 2 tablespoons of butter over a medium heat
- Stir in the lemon juice, mushrooms and salt into the pan.
- Cook for 3 to 5 minutes, until the mushrooms have become soft
- Using a slotted scoop, remove the mushrooms from the liquid and place them in a small bowl
- Cook the spinach in the microwave for two minutes
- Put the spinach into the lemon / butter liquid and cook on a high heat for three minutes
- Stir the mushrooms back into the pan with the spinach
- Stir in the Spirulina and remove from the heat

- Using a spoon, remove the fat from the top of the liquid in the large frying pan with the chicken
- In a mixing bowl, whisk the milk and the flour together until well blended
- Stir in the horseradish.
- Stir the milk mixture into the pan with the chicken
- Mix in the sunflower seeds and cook until the sauce starts to become thicker
- Pour the spinach mixture into a serving dish, then arrange the chicken on top.
- Use the lemon slices as a garnish

* Healthy Options: Substitute crispy fried onions for the lemons as a garnish

This main dish serves four (4) people.

WHITE AND GREEN STUFFED MANICOTTI

- 2 – 26 Ounce Jars of Spaghetti Sauce
- 2 Boxes of Manicotti
- 2 Chicken Breasts, Cooked and Finely Chopped
- 1/2 Small White Onion, Minced
- 1/4 Pound of Fresh Spinach
- 1 Small Package of Sliced Mozzarella Cheese
- 1 Cup Ricotta Cheese
- 2/3 Cup of Heavy Cream, Whipped
- 1/4 Cup Fresh Grated Parmesan Cheese
- 1/4 Cup of Fresh Parsley, Finely Chopped
- 2 Tablespoons of Earthrise® Spirulina
- 1/4 Cup of Olive Oil
- 1/2 teaspoon of Salt
- 1/2 teaspoon of Ground Black Pepper
- 1/2 teaspoon of Nutmeg, Finely Grated

- Preheat the oven to 375°
- In a large frying pan, sauté the onions in the oil until they are slightly browned
- Cook the spinach in the microwave for two minutes, then place it into the frying pan, mixing well
- Mix all of the other items, except the spaghetti sauce and Earthrise® Spirulina, into the spinach mixture
- Carefully mix the Spirulina into the mixture
- Using a tablespoon, stuff the uncooked manicotti with the spinach mixture
- Cover the bottom of a large baking pan with some of the spaghetti sauce
- Arrange the stuffed manicotti on the spaghetti sauce (the pasta should not touch)
- Pour the rest of the spaghetti sauce over the manicotti
- Arrange the sliced mozzarella cheese over the manicotti
- Cover the pan with aluminum foil
- Bake the dish for 1 hour

* Healthy Options: As an option, sprinkle shredded sharp cheddar cheese over the mixture in place of the mozzarella cheese,

This main dish serves six to eight (6-8) people.

DOUBLE DECKER FISH FILLETS

- 2 Medium Eggs
- 1 Pound of Potatoes
- 1 Pound of Salmon, De-boned
- 1 Pound of Bread Crumbs
- 1 Medium Lemon, Juiced
- 1/4 Clove of Garlic, Finely Chopped
- 2 Tablespoons of Green Onion, Chopped
- 1-1/2 Tablespoons of Earthrise® Spirulina
- 1 Tablespoon of Fennel, Finely Chopped
- 1 teaspoon of Ground Black Pepper
- 1/2 teaspoon of Salt
- 1/8 teaspoon of Cloves, Finely Ground

- Cook the potatoes in the microwave (about 10 minutes per potato)
- Peel and mash with some salt, pepper, butter and a bit of milk
- Cook the fish until pink all of the way through (using a frying pan with some oil would be the quickest)
- Mash the fish
- Put all of the ingredients, except for the potato, the eggs and the bread crumbs, into a large mixing bowl and combine until fully mixed
- Divide the potatoes and the fish mixture each into 12 portions
- Take each portion of potato and form it into a round disk, about ½" thick
- Place a portion of fish into the center of each potato disk and bring the edges of the disk up so it forms a ball around the fish
- Fill a medium saucepan with enough oil to fill the pan up about 2 inches and place over a high heat
- Beat the eggs in a medium bowl
- Dip each ball into the egg wash and coat entirely with some bread crumbs
- Deep fry until golden brown, carefully dropping each ball into the hot oil for a few minutes each ball

This main dish serves six (6) people.

CHICKEN SPIRULINA

- 2 Large Chicken Breasts, Boneless
- 1 Large Carrot
- 1 Green Onion, Chopped
- 1 Cup of Light Cream (Half & Half)
- 1 Cup of Warm Water
- 3 Tablespoons of Flour
- 1 Tablespoon Oil
- 1 Tablespoon Butter
- 1 Tablespoon of Earthrise® Spirulina
- 1-1/2 teaspoons Paprika
- 1/2 teaspoon of Salt
- 1/2 teaspoon of Ground Black Pepper

- Peel the carrots and slice into thin circles
- In a saucepan, heat the water over a high heat to cook the carrots
- Cut each chicken breast in half (remove white tendon) and cut each piece in half
- Using a kitchen mallet, pound each piece until about ½" thick
- In a shallow bowl, mix the flour, salt and the pepper
- Coat the chicken pieces with the flour mixture
- In a large frying pan, heat the olive oil and butter
- Cook the chicken pieces until lightly browned on all sides. Add additional butter and / or olive oil if needed
- Move the chicken to a serving dish
- Turn the heat to medium and cook the onions until soft
- Add the paprika and cook for 1 minute
- Add the half and half while stirring constantly
- Cook for 3 – 5 minutes until it gets thicker
- Turn off the heat and add the Spirulina, whisking vigorously
- Pour the sauce over the chicken and garnish with the carrot strips

This main dish serves four (4) people.

LIVING PASTA SAUCE

- 1 Fresh Garlic Clove
- 1/2 Cup Parmesan Cheese, grated
- 1/4 Cup Virgin Olive Oil
- 1/4 Cup Butter
- 1 Tablespoon Fresh Cilantro,
- 1 Tablespoon Earthrise® Spirulina
- 1 Tablespoon Basil
- 1/2 teaspoon Fresh Lemon Juice

- Combine all of the ingredients into a blender
- Blend until smooth and creamy
- Pour mixture into a saucepan
- Heat over a medium heat until warm (do NOT boil)

* Healthy Options: Serve over fresh vegetables.

This dish serves four (4) people.\

PASTA DEL SPIRULENE

- 2 Eggs
- 1-3/4 Cup Whole Wheat Flour or Durum Wheat Semolina
- 1/8 Cup Parmesan Cheese, Grated
- 2 Tablespoons Earthrise® Spirulina
- 1 Tablespoon Garlic Butter
- 1 Dash Salt
- 1 Dash Pepper

- Mix the flour, Spirulina, salt, pepper and cheese in a mixing bowl
- Dig a hole in the center of the mixture and ad the eggs and 2 tablespoons of water, mixing by hand
- Add additional water, a little at a time until the dough is stiff but pliable
- Put the dough onto a floured surface and kneed until very stiff
- Process the dough either by hand or with a pasta machine
    - Pasta Machine – follow the instructions of the machine
    - By Hand
        - Roll until the dough is in very thin sheets
        - Hang until no longer tacky
        - Cut into thin strips
- Heat water in a large pot until boiling
- Cook the pasta for 5 – 10 minutes (depending on preference)
- Serve with garlic butter

* Healthy Options: Serve with Living Pasta Sauce

This main dish serves four (4) people.

TOFU CUTLETS

- 1 Package – Firm Tofu
- 1 Fresh Lemon, Juice Only
- 3 Tablespoons Tamari
- 2 teaspoons Garlic Granules
- 1 teaspoon Earthrise® Spirulina

- Preheat the oven to 350
- Slice the tofu lengthwise into ½" thick slices.
- Lay the slices on a lightly oiled cookie sheet
- Combine the remaining ingredients well and pour over the tofu slices
- Bake for 15 minutes
- Serve in a sandwich

* Healthy Options: Serve with Tofu Gravy

This dish offers four (4) servings.

SWEETS AND TREATS

(We saved the best for last!)

Earthrise® Spirulina helps to strengthen the immune system.*

* These statements have not been evaluated by the Food and Drug Administration. This product is not intended to diagnose, treat, cure or prevent disease.

ICE CREAM SPIRULINA

- 1/2 Pound of Granulated Sugar
- 1/4 Quart Cream
- 2 Tablespoons Earthrise® Spirulina

- Mix all of the ingredients together
- Set in a double boiler until scalded
- Freeze

This desert offers approximately six (6) servings.

PISTACHIO SPIRULINA ICE CREAM

- 1 Banana, Finely Chopped
- 1/4 Pound of Fresh Pistachios
- 1/4 Quart of Cream
- 1 Tablespoon of Earthrise® Spirulina

- To blanch: simply plunge food (usually vegetables and fruits) into boiling waters briefly, then into cold water to stop the cooking process. It loosens the skin (as with peaches and tomatoes) so it peels easily and also sets the color and flavor (as with veggies) before freezing.
- Boil some water in a small pot
- Blanch the pistachios by boiling them for thirty seconds
- Remove them from the boiling water and soak in ice water for two minutes
- Remove the skins from the pistachios
- Using a food processor or mortar / pestle, grind the pistachios into a fine paste
- Mix the paste with the cream and the Spirulina
- Pass the mixture through a sieve
- Freeze for several hours

This desert offers approximately four (4) servings.

BANANA ENERGY BARS

- 4 Ripe Bananas, Mashed
- 1 Cup Sunflower Seeds Coarsely Ground
- 1 Cup Shredded Coconut
- 1/2 Cup Raisins (Soaked in water for a while)
- 1/2 Cup Tahini
- 4 Tablespoons Soy Milk Powder
- 2 Tablespoons Lecithin
- 2 teaspoons Earthrise® Spirulina
- 1 teaspoon Vanilla Extract

- Combine all ingredients (except ½ cup coconut) in a mixing bowl
- Using a spoon, form the mixture into balls
- Roll the balls into the remaining coconut
- Place the balls on a flat sheet an cover with plastic
- Chill at least one hour

Healthy Options: Use Almond butter in place of the tahini

This desert offers approximately eight (8) servings.

SPIRALOONS

- 4 Cups Shredded Coconut
- 1 Cup Slice Almonds
- 1-1/3 Cup Maple Syrup
- 2/3 Cup Barley Flour
- 1 Tablespoons Earthrise® Spirulina
- 2 teaspoons Almond Extract
- 1/2 teaspoon Sea Salt

- Preheat the oven to 350
- Combine the ingredients in a large mixing bowl
- Using a tablespoon, scoop the mixture into small balls and place on a non-stick baking sheet
- Using the edge of the spoon, make an "X" on the top of each ball (should be at least ¼" deep into the ball)
- Bake for 10 minutes

This desert offers approximately forty (40) cookies.

3.5 BILLION YEAR BARS

- 1 Cup Unsalted Peanuts
- 1 Cup Carob Powder
- 1 Cup Honey
- 1 Cup Cashew Butter
- 1/2 Cup Toasted Sesame Seeds
- 2 Tablespoons Earthrise® Spirulina

- Melt the almond butter and honey over a low heat, constantly stirring
- When blended, stir in the carob powder, sesame seeds and Spirulina
- Blend well
- Pour into a rectangular pan
- Refrigerate at least 1-½ to 2 hours
- Cut into bars (approximately 2" by 4" and wrap each bar in plastic

Healthy Options: Substitute Almond Butter for the Cashew Butter

This desert offers approximately ten to twelve (10-12) servings.

NUTTY SWEET COOKIES

- 1 Cup of Shredded Dry Coconut
- 1 Cup of Walnuts, Crushed
- 1 Cup of Raisins
- 1 Cup of Semi-Sweet Chocolate Chips
- 1 Cup of Pure Maple Syrup
- 1 Cup of Flour
- 1/2 Cup of Vegetable Oil
- 2 Tablespoons of Earthrise® Spirulina
- 1/2 teaspoon of Baking Soda

- Preheat the oven to 350°
- Mix the oil and the syrup together until well blended
- Add the flour, soda, Spirulina and the coconut, mixing until well blended
- Add the other ingredients, mixing until well blended
- Grease a baking sheet
- Form small balls, about 1" in diameter and place on the baking sheet, about 2" apart
- Bake for 15 to 20 minutes, until browned

Healthy Options: Substitute carob chips in place of the chocolate chips.

This desert offers approximately three (3) dozen servings

N

P

Q

S

T

V

W

About the Author

Lance S. Sigal is the Director of Marketing, which includes the Education team, for Earthrise Nutritionals, LLC. With over 24 years of experience in sales and marketing, his work with various products and sales channels has given him a unique insight into the retail marketplace and a keen understanding of the dynamic needs of consumers.

Lance is devoted to raising the visibility of Spirulina and its advantages, especially as Earthrise celebrates its 25th anniversary in 2005. Believing that education is a never ending process in life, he has combined this principle with an in-depth knowledge of Spirulina to help teach people about the unique benefits of this simple green powder. This comprehensive cookbook is a part of that effort with the goal of enabling people to incorporate Spirulina into their individual diet and health regimens.

About the Cover Illustrator

David O'Connell is an award winning graphic designer and art director who has been engaged in a wide variety of creative assignments since graduating from the California Institute of the Arts. David headed up his own design firm, Canyon Design, for 16 years before becoming the Creative Director at the Young Company, a leading B-to-B advertising agency specializing in high technology accounts. He is currently an Art Director for The Phelps Group, an integrated marketing communications agency based in Santa Monica, California.

Printed in the United States
26131LVS00006B/91-150

INDEX